INCREASE YOUR WORTH:

MAKE MORE, GIVE MORE, LIVE MORE

Copyright © 2021 Warren Stickney

All rights reserved.

The characters and events portrayed in this book are fictitious. Any similarity to real persons, living or dead, is coincidental and not intended by the author.

No part of this book may be reproduced, or stored in a retrieval system, or transmitted in any form or by any means, electronic, mechanical, photocopying, recording, or otherwise, without express written permission of the publisher.

*Tell me, what is it you plan to do
with your one wild and precious life?*

—*Mary Oliver*

FOREWORD

Growing up I was dyslexic and had a very tough time reading anything. I vividly remember my sister Lindy, my mother and father reading *Horton Hears a Who* and *The Little Engine that Could*. These childhood stories had a significant impact on my worldview and indeed, as Horton says, **"a person's a person no matter how small"** but when we all come together, we can accomplish huge things and indeed be heard.

I want to dedicate this book to my children for whom I wish a better future. And with a little help from all of us, it will be a better world to live in than what we have experienced. I also dedicate it to my fantastic team and to Jeannie, who has encouraged me to embark on this project and has given me the strength and confidence to assist many, many others in realizing their dreams and impacting so many important causes. And lastly, I dedicate this to my clients who have adopted these strategies and indeed use the tax savings to build schools, medical clinics, support education and the homeless, cancer research, and countless other important endeavors, where all it took was a little bit of encouragement.

Additionally, I give my thanks to the Snowmass Chapel and the Aspen Institute; Snowmass chapel for its broad and welcoming worldview of helping so many regardless of who they are or where they're from and the Aspen Institute which has convened many from around the world to open their eyes and see what was beyond their vision. TED and their conferences have continued to be a spark of inspiration in bringing educational curiosity to the masses. I want to also recognize and thank the Million Dollar Round Table and my friends and colleagues there who dedicate their lives to helping others.

TABLE OF CONTENTS

Foreword
Introduction
Chapter 1
   A Note from the Author
   Discussion Questions
Chapter 2
   A Note from the Author
   Discussion Questions
Chapter 3
   A Note from the Author
   Discussion Questions
Chapter 4
   A Note from the Author
   Discussion Questions
Chapter 5
   A Note from the Author
   Discussion *Questions*
Chapter 6
   A Note from the Author
   The Big Question
Conclusion
Resources

INTRODUCTION

What kind of difference do you want to make?

We all want to make a difference. Whether that is in our own lives, in the lives of our family and friends, in our community, or across the world – we all want to leave a positive impact on the people and places that matter most to us.

The question is, how do we leave the greatest impact?

In this book, you will meet characters who face this exact question. Although the characters are fictional, they represent financial situations that are commonplace in today's world. And they are faced with an issue that is vital and yet not widely discussed:

After you have reached a certain level of material wealth and success – what happens next?

The mission of this book is to show you the possibilities that exist through charitable giving. Throughout this story, you will learn how directing your wealth through different methods of charitable giving will allow you to control your assets, support the people and groups that you value most, and make a lasting impact on the world.

What You Will Find

While reading this book, you will learn different strategies that you can employ to establish tax-deductible trusts and foundations. At the end of each chapter, you will find helpful points from the chapter as well as discussion questions. These questions are designed to continue the conversation and help you as you continue on your financial planning journey.

At the end of the book, there is a special 'Resources' chapter which will give you clear and informative details about each of the charitable giving methods discussed in the book. You can also learn more anytime by visiting www.IncreaseYourWorth.org.

Each of us is given only one life. One opportunity to make something for ourselves, for our families, and for the people who need us.

When we live for ourselves, when we worry only about what we can accumulate and how we will benefit, we will never be satisfied. There is always something else that we don't have. And there is always something to lose. We will become very small in the world. But when we live for others, when we make service a part of who we are – we will find that our lives grow and grow ... and we will never be without purpose. There is always something else that we can do. There is always someone else who needs us.

The same is true for our wealth when we only focus on how much we have. When you give your wealth to the government through taxes, you lose any ability to determine how or where those funds are used.

Charitable giving empowers you to have a direct influence on the causes and people that are closest to your heart. That is what *Increase Your Worth* is all about.

May this book find you well, and may it enable you to make a profound difference in the world around you.

CHAPTER 1

It was two in the morning and Scott couldn't sleep again. It was becoming a regular occurrence now, rising in the dark and sitting on the side of the bed, listening to his wife Carol breathe deeply, the rest of the house silent. He sat for a moment longer, steadying his own breathing, letting his heartbeat slow, and then he stood and walked through the dark house like a ghost. In the hallway were two doors, each one leading to a bedroom.

He carefully opened the first and peered inside, where a soft light glowed and he could just make out the peacefully sleeping form of his thirteen-year-old daughter, Emily. He stood in the doorway for a moment, watching a book rising and falling on Emily's chest, and then he quietly entered the room and lifted it from her, found the bookmark on her bedside table, and set it down.

He closed her door quietly and walked to the next door, where his younger daughter, eleven-year-old Savannah, was tangled up in a mass of blankets. Her sleep was always more intense, more in line with her spirited personality. Books and toys and her clothes littered the floor. He would have to remind her in the morning to pick those things up, keep her room tidy for at least an hour or two before she tore it apart again. She was always involved in some fantasy game, some experiment, always wanting to investigate and learn – and she rarely had time for cleaning up.

Scott closed the door to her room and walked the rest of the hall, passing the front door and entering the kitchen. In the dark he opened the refrigerator door and looked around, but he could find nothing that he wanted. He closed the door and the blue light and cool air snapped away, and he stood in the dark.

What was he waiting for? Why was he awake, again, in the middle of the night? When the world slept and his family slept, and he roamed the house, his eyes tired but his mind very much alive, turning over and over again the same questions of time and the future.

He walked into the front room and lay on the couch, staring at the ceiling. Without looking he could sense the red glow of the digital clock across the room beneath the television, and he knew that soon it would be three, then four, then the dark would slowly turn gray and then blue, the sun slowly rising again and it would be time to go back to work.

Scott was 49 years old. He worked as an executive at New Wave Technologies, and the company recently announced that they were going public. This was a monumental change for both the company and Scott. For decades, he had been holding stock options.

Now that New Wave was going public, those stock options would have to be exercised before they expired. If he missed the expiration date, they would lose their value.

It should have been a happy time for Scott and his family. After all, his stock options, once exercised, would yield over $5 million. That, along with his salary, afforded him choices that he never thought would be possible in his lifetime. But instead of making him happy, putting him at ease, these choices were causing him greater and greater amounts of stress. Because no matter how many times he turned ideas over in his mind, he didn't know what to *do* with this new wealth. And in three months, he was going to be faced with a tax burden that threatened to wipe out a significant amount. Just like that – gone.

So now he was awake again, thinking again, trying to determine the best course of action for his family. For his daughters, and for their families someday. Now that he had acquired undreamed-of wealth, he was so scared of losing it that he couldn't sleep at night. As soon as he exercised his stock options, they would become regular income – and taxed accordingly. Nearly 40% would go to Uncle Sam. There had to be a better way, he thought. But as much as he tried, as many nights as he had stayed awake and researched and considered different scenarios, he could not reach a conclusion that felt right.

And if he did nothing ...

His heart rate rose again and he stood from the couch and walked out the back door onto his deck. The cool night air covered his face and there was a sweetness in the breeze that was a comfort to him. He breathed deeply. Beyond his back fence, the world of his neighborhood disappeared and the ground dropped in a steep decline, creating a beautiful vista over miles and miles of wildland.

At night he could make out on the shadows of the trees in the distance, but from far below came the sound of running water, a creek dancing over rocks and fallen tree limbs, and the trees themselves whispered to each other in the night.

Scott breathed deeply and closed his eyes.

You will be okay, he said to himself. You will figure this out. Just relax, breathe, and think.

He opened his eyes. Movement from next door caused him to turn and when he looked, he could see the silhouette of a man standing on his own deck, staring out at the same expanse of wildland.

Bill Jones.

"Great," Scott said to himself.

He walked inside and closed the door.

*

The next day was Friday, and Scott came home from work, ready to relax and maybe spend some time during the weekend planning his next move. Carol was sitting on the couch when he walked through the door, and from down the hall came the sounds of music playing from Emily's room. Her room was always meticulously neat and organized, which meant the girls always used her room when they wanted to hang out.

Guided Giving

FINDING YOUR CHARITABLE FOCUS

INTRODUCTION

Choosing where to focus your charitable giving can be deeply personal and, at times, overwhelming. You want your contributions to reflect who you are, what you care about, and the values that drive you. This guide is here to help you navigate that journey by tapping into your motivations and passions. Together, we'll explore the causes that truly resonate with you, revisit the moments where you've made a difference, and craft a focus statement that speaks to your heart. From there, you'll learn how to find and support organizations that align with your values, ensuring that your generosity creates a meaningful and lasting impact.

"Martha Jones stopped by," Carol said.

She stood and greeted Scott and they walked into the kitchen together, where Scott poured himself a glass of water.

Scott did not immediately answer. Anything to do with the Jones family was not his concern – he intentionally stayed out of their affairs, never asking questions, never saying too much. The truth was, he could not stand Bill Jones.

Finally, the silence stretched on for long enough that he settled himself down at the kitchen table and sighed.

"And what did Martha Jones want?" He asked.

"Invited us over to dinner tomorrow," Carol said. "Bill asked for you specifically."

"Why would he do that?"

"I don't know," Carol said, trying to hide a smile. "Maybe he likes you."

Scott shook his head and drank more water.

"All I want to do this weekend is relax," he said. "And there is no way I can relax when we are having dinner with Bill Jones."

"I don't understand why you can't just give him a chance," Carol said. "They are lovely people."

"There is nothing lovely about Bill Jones," Scott said. "This is a man who has it all, and who is never afraid to show it off. My god – how many parties can you throw? But there they are, almost every weekend, another group of people waltzing through the door."

"He is a people person," Carol said. "He has always been pleasant with me."

"Of course he is!" Scott said. "When life comes that easy to you, when you have it all, when you are so rich…"

He stopped himself for a moment, recovering with a drink of water.

"You know what? I have enough going on right now without some dinner with Bill Jones, without him throwing all his success in my face. Thanks for the invite, but I'll pass."

He stood abruptly and went to the refrigerator to refill his glass.

"That's too bad," Carol said casually. "Because I already said we would love to be there."

*

Saturday night arrived and Scott and Carol walked next door to Jones Manor. Although there were no signs indicating that anywhere on the property, that was the name Scott had assigned it, both in his mind and privately with Carol.

It was a looming home, two stories, with a dazzling front porch framed by dramatic white pillars, and on each side, windows glowing with light, so that the home always looked alive, warm, inviting. Walking by at night, visitors would notice the stark contrast between Jones Manor and the modest home immediately next door, as though a benevolent king had allowed one of his lowly subjects to set up a house under his watchful eye. At certain times of day, the sun was positioned in just the right place so that Jones Manor cast a deep shadow on Scott's home.

Martha Jones welcomed them at the door and gratefully accepted a bottle of wine from Carol, and the two of them walked inside together like old friends while Scott trailed behind. He had never been inside Jones Manor – Carol and Martha had been friends for some time and Carol had come to the house on several occasions, but Scott was stepping inside for the first time.

It was like walking into a richly appointed museum. Ornate décor, a beautiful crystal chandelier in the entryway, exquisite artwork on the walls, and a dramatic staircase just inside the entry that led to more rooms. Off to one side was the kitchen and beyond that, the dining room. Scott followed the talking women as though in trance, and just before they stepped into the dining room, he glanced to his left and saw one more room – a beautiful library, filled from floor to ceiling with books.

Inside the dining room was Bill Jones, who walked over, smiling. He was older than Scott, in his mid-60s, but kept a trim figure and a casually combed back head of full silver hair. Most striking were his green eyes, which fired with energy and enthusiasm, and which now shined brightly while he held out his hand to Scott.

"So glad you could make it tonight!" He said. "I have been wanting to talk with you for some time now."

"Yes, well," Scott said. "You know, work keeps us pretty busy."

Bill held up a hand.

"Say no more, my friend. I know exactly how that goes."

I doubt it, Scott thought, but he was determined to make the best of the situation. After all, he was a guest in their home for the evening. And he had dealt with worse characters at the office. He could tolerate anyone for a few hours.

After a bit more casual conversation, it was time to sit down for dinner. The two couples made their way to their seats around the dining table, which was tastefully arranged with beautiful gold rimmed plates and crystal glasses, filled now with wine. On the menu were deliciously seared pork chops covered in a sweet and sour sauce made from fresh figs and grapes cooked in balsamic vinegar and honey, and then offset by a light radicchio salad.

It's perfect, of course, Scott thought as he tasted each bite. Despite his best efforts, he couldn't argue that this was one of the best meals he had eaten in some time. With work and the stress over his upcoming decision, he most often ate something at his office desk or on the drive home – he had not been out to dinner in months, and now, tasting this incredible meal, he felt the pull of regret.

The others were talking and now Scott returned to the present moment to listen to the conversation.

"We are just so appreciative that you invited us over," Carol was saying. "I cannot remember the last meal I had that was this delicious."

"It is our pleasure," Martha said. "I recently started discovering new recipes to try, and I love having people over to taste them. This one happens to be one of Bill's favorites."

Bill looked up with a half-smile, nodding vigorously while he finished chewing a mouthful of food.

"She spoils me," he said finally. "She does the work and I gain all the benefits!"

"You two seem so content," Carol said. "It is amazing, really. Every time I come over here, I get the impression that you are perfectly content in your lives."

"Oh, it wasn't always that way," Martha said, sending a knowing glance over toward Bill. "But we have come a long way in our lives, and we are determined to make the most of our time while we have it on this earth."

Bill smiled and raised his glass.

"That sounds like a toast, right there," he said. Holding his glass a bit higher toward the center of the table, he said:

> *"Wine comes in at the mouth*
> *And love comes in at the eye;*
> *That's all we shall know for truth*
> *Before we grow old and die.*
> *I lift the glass to my mouth,*
> *I look at you, and I sigh."*

They all raised their glasses and the soft clink of crystal filled the air and they drank together.

Setting her glass down, Carol said, "That was beautiful. Where did you hear that?"

"William Butler Yeats," Bill said.

"He is always looking for an excuse to show off," Martha joked. "He has that library filled with books and just has to let you know what he has been reading!"

Always showing off, Scott thought, swallowing another mouthful of wine. I am not surprised at all.

"I hate to admit this, but we have not had much time for reading lately," Carol said. "We are both so busy with work, and then with this recent decision that Scott is facing …"

She stopped for a moment and looked at Scott, then she took a drink of wine.

"Anyway," she continued. "It would be nice to have something nice to read again."

"I would be happy to recommend something to you," Martha said. "Before you leave."

"What decision do you have to make?" Bill asked.

Scott looked up from his meal to see Bill's bright green eyes piercing into him. Of course he would ask that question, he thought. Just another chance for him to prove how much better he is than everyone else.

"It's nothing, really," Scott said. "A financial decision, that's all."

Bill nodded thoughtfully. His eyes never left Scott, and eventually Scott dropped his gaze and studied the remaining fragments of his pork chop.

"He has been working for thirty years at the same tech firm," Carol answered for him. "Since he was a teenager, really. Started on the ground floor when they first opened their doors."

"That is admirable," Martha said. "Loyalty is hard to come by these days."

Scott nodded an acknowledgement while Carol continued her story.

"So when he began, he was not paid a large salary – however, they offered him stock options as part of his total compensation package, which he accepted. Well, over the past three decades, that firm has steadily grown and grown, and in recent years it exploded in size, acquiring several other firms in the state."

"So those stocks are worth quite a bit now," Martha concluded.

"Exactly," Carol said. "At the same time, our combined salaries have grown considerably and have made it possible for us to live very comfortably. So, this year, the company announced they were going public. Which means –"

"Which means those stock options are about to make you a very wealthy man," Bill said.

He had a curious look on his face. Normally, people would smile when talking about a potential windfall. But Bill was not smiling. Scott could not exactly understand what the look meant. It was almost as though … as though Bill felt sorry for him.

"How marvelous!" Martha said. "And what are you going to do with that wealth?"

"That is the problem," Carol said. "We took all these steps, and now here we are and we don't know what to *do*. And now we have only a few months left to decide before we lose it to taxes."

Martha sighed and took a drink of wine, looking over her glass at Bill as though to prompt him.

"That sounds like a tough decision," Bill said. His eyes still had not left Scott's.

"It will be fine," Scott said, but his voice lacked all conviction. He finished his wine and said, "You all don't want to hear about our troubles, I'm sure. It is just a decision."

"A very important one," Bill said. "A life-altering one."

"Right," Scott said. He started to speak again but then stopped and stared at his plate.

Several moments passed in silence. Then Bill finally smiled and addressed Scott again.

"You know what? I have this new telescope out back that I have been waiting all day to use. Would you like to join me, Scott?"

Scott looked first at his wife and then at Martha, who was smiling at him as well. He had no choice, really. It was either go with Bill or run screaming from Jones Manor.

"Sure," Scott said. "Let's go."

*

Outside, the night air was clean and cool. Spring was in full season and the sweet smells of the trees and the coolness rising off the water far below was enough to put Scott at ease despite his current situation. Bill walked across the wood deck and pulled a cover off his telescope, a large and elaborately designed machine that looked like it could have come from NASA itself.

He removed the lens cap and peered through the eyepiece, making small adjustments, standing back to look at the sky, and then returning again to the eyepiece. Finally, he stood back and smiled at Scott.

"Come look at this," he said.

Scott crossed the deck and bent over the telescope, dipping one side of his face to peer into the eyepiece. Inside he saw a shockingly large image of the moon, so close that he could make out its features, it hills and crevices, every small shift in land. He stood back and looked at the night sky, where the moon shined bright like a perfect glowing orb, and then he looked back into the telescope and saw the intricate details again.

"Wow," he said.

"Amazing, isn't it?" Bill said. "Incredible what we are able to see just by changing our perspective. Sometimes we just need the right tools."

Scott stepped away from the telescope and gazed out over the wildland. From the blue-black tree shadows came the calls of birds in the darkening night.

"This is my favorite place to be," Bill said. "I come out here whenever I need to think, or just get away and breathe for a while."

Why would you need to get away from your perfect life? Scott thought.

"There is so much to see out here," Bill continued. "And now with my telescope I can gaze up at the stars. You know, in my youth I wanted to be a ship captain. Using the stars to guide my ship home."

"Really?"

Bill stepped away from his telescope and stared into the distance.

"The natural world has a lot to teach us if we can stop and listen."

They were silent for a moment, listening to the gentle swaying whisper of thousands of trees below.

"I've seen you out here some nights," Bill said. He turned and faced Scott. "I am a bit of a restless sleeper myself."

Finally, Scott could no longer resist speaking up. This whole night, from the moment he walked into Jones Manor until right then, standing on the back deck and listening to Bill talk about how *I am just like you* – it was suddenly too much.

"I don't get it," Scott blurted out. "Your life is so perfect! If I were you, I would be sleeping easy every day of my life on my perfect bed inside my perfect mansion after eating a perfect meal! How can you possibly lose sleep?"

Bill laughed in an understanding way and looked at the stars again.

"I can tell you the secret, if you want to hear it," he said.

"What secret?"

"Do you read often, Scott?"

"I don't really have the time for that."

"I'm reading right now the life of Ben Franklin. How he was able to change the world *and* help himself at the same time."

"What are you talking about?"

"Here is the secret. Scott, you should give it away."

"What?"

"Give it away."

"Have you lost your mind? I am trying to keep my wealth, not lose it."

"What if I told you there was a way that you could keep your wealth, even grow it, and do a lot of good for the things you care most about?"

"That seems impossible …"

Bill put the lens cap back on his telescope and gently pulled the cover over it. He motioned toward the wooden chairs that were set up to face out toward the wildland.

"Scott, let's sit out here a while," he said. "I want to tell you a story of how I learned to do well by doing good."

MR. WARREN B STICKNEY

A Note from the Author

At the end of each chapter, you will find useful summaries (like you see below) as well as questions to guide your understanding of the chapter's main themes. Please feel free to use the space provided in the book to answer the questions and make notes.

Countless individuals find themselves in situations similar to Scott's. With companies going public on a daily basis, it becomes crucial for you to take action and exercise your stock options before they expire, ensuring you maximize your potential gains.

It's important to note that exercising stock options comes with tax implications. By exercising your stock options, they will be subject to taxation as ordinary income. Understanding the tax implications and planning accordingly can help you make informed decisions and minimize potential tax burdens.

Fortunately, there's a way to make a positive impact while also benefiting from tax advantages. Charitable giving presents a remarkable opportunity to contribute to causes that hold significant meaning for you while earning valuable tax deductions. It's a win-win situation that allows you to support the causes closest to your heart while also optimizing your financial situation.

When it comes to charitable giving, two widely recognized structures are the charitable lead trust (CLT) and the charitable remainder trust (CRT). These structures offer distinct benefits and can be tailored to align with your specific philanthropic goals. Exploring these options with the guidance of a financial advisor or estate planning professional can empower you to create a lasting impact while maximizing the advantages of charitable giving.

Whether you're navigating stock options, considering tax implications, or seeking to make a difference through charitable giving, understanding these concepts and exploring available strategies can position you for financial success and meaningful contributions to the causes you care about.

Discussion Questions

1. What does success mean to you?

2. What are your three core values, and how do they relate to your definition of success?

CHAPTER 2

"Have you spent much time on the East Coast, Scott?"

"Not much, why?"

"Good friends of mine live out there – for generations they owned a large beach resort up in Maine, near Acadia. Can you imagine that? What it must feel like to have your own resort, to put your feet in the Atlantic. Paradise, I tell you."

"Where are you going with this, Bill?"

Bill smiled. Scott was beginning to learn that this was what he did any time he wanted to share good news with someone.

"I am telling you this because I once was right where you were, Scott. A lot of wealth and no idea what to do with it. Scared of losing it all the time. Wanting to make sure I used it right."

He paused.

"Lot of responsibility comes with wealth, Scott. That's something they don't tell you growing up. Lot of decisions to be made."

He turned to look out at the wildland, as though considering something. For a long time, they sat in silence except for the sounds coming from the shadows beyond the back fence. Finally, Bill turned back to Scott.

"But as I was saying, this beach resort. Belongs to friends of ours. A place they call Hearthstone Harbor. Do you know why they call it that?"

"Bill, this is the first time I have heard that name in my life. I have no idea why they would name it Hearthstone Harbor or anything else."

Bill laughed.

"Okay, okay, I am not telling this right. Let me start at the beginning. This was back in the late 1800s, when a man by the name of Alexander Tremble bought some property on the shores of Maine and built a cabin for himself and his family. Built it himself, can you believe that?"

Scott tried to imagine building anything with his bare hands. Although he was handy enough to fix little things in the house – leaking pipes, a garbage disposal that suddenly quit working, relighting the pilot on the water heater, replacing a few panels on the wood fence – he could not fathom the skill and frankly the courage it would take to build up a house out of the ground.

"So, he built this log cabin on the waterfront," Bill said. "And then he had some friends in the area, and they all wanted to come out to the water in the summers too, so you know what he did? He built a few bungalows for them, too! And just like that, you have the beginning of a property forming. Imagine having a waterfront cabin where you can spend all the quality time you want with the people you love most – and then next door you have your best friends showing up. Imagine the times they must have had out there!"

"As much as I am enjoying this story, I fail to see how it applies to my situation," Scott said. As soon as he said the words, he was surprised by how regretful he felt. Within a few short hours, he was finding himself less angry at Bill Jones. Still, the man had a way of talking on and on and on – and what was the point?

"Of course, of course!" Bill said. "We are getting to that part, I promise. I'm sorry, I love history, and I love hearing the stories of people creating these incredible and lasting things where nothing existed before. I am interested in legacy, as I am sure you are, Scott. Something tells me that is part of what keeps you up at night."

Scott did not respond to this. He didn't want Bill to know how close he was to the truth.

"Let me just give you a little more history of Hearthstone Harbor, if you don't mind," he said. "It will help you understand everything that came later, I promise."

"All right, Bill," Scott said. "Please continue."

Bill smiled, clearly gleeful to proceed with his story.

"So, there they were, the cabin, the bungalows. All their close friends and family spending time together. Now, there was more than one way to access Hearthstone Harbor. The first was by steamer, traveling to the Bar Harbor ferry landing. This was popular for a time but most people were traveling by land to access the summer homes. So more often than not, they would come by train to the Bar Harbor Station. Of course, that would not get you all the way there, so enterprising local farmers made a steady income transporting visitors up the coast to Hearthstone Harbor by horse and carriage. Can you believe that, Scott?"

"Sounds like a long trip," Scott said.

"Exactly!" Bill said. "Exactly! It was a journey to reach Hearthstone Harbor! And in that time, it was a transformation, too! Imagine leaving your home in the city, traveling by train, arriving at a small station, where a carriage was waiting to carry you the rest of the way. Imagine how long that must have taken to reach Hearthstone Harbor, how thankful they must have been to finally arrive, the feeling of accomplishment when they carried their luggage into their summer bungalow and announced, we have arrived! Imagine sitting outside that first night, far away from where you have been, far away from any of the stress and difficulty of life back in the city. Just you, your family, your friends, and the beauty of nature that surrounds you."

Despite his best efforts, Scott found himself being pulled further and further into Bill's story. He imagined what it would be like to leave New Wave Technologies, to pack up his bags and meet Carol and the girls at the station, to travel for miles and miles, the city receding in the distance, a train racing along the tracks like a time machine leaving behind all memories and stresses and transporting them into a place that exists in a different realm altogether, arriving to find a helpful horseman waiting for them, and a carriage, loading their luggage heavily into the back. Feeling the bounce and pull of the carriage as they rattled slowly down newly formed paths and roads, farther and farther away from the world they once knew, until at last they arrived, safe and sound, where they belonged. The first breath of fresh air, the cool salty smell of the water, the soft lapping of tide on the shore, the trees …

"Still with me, Scott?"

"Pardon?"

Scott shook his head and looked up. Bill was smiling at him.

"You went away there for a moment. Everything all right?"

"Yes, yes, of course," Scott said, clearing his mind. "Of course. I was just … thinking."

Bill smiled again.

"I do that a lot," he said.

"So you were saying, about the train and the carriage?"

"Yes," Bill said. "So, they started with the one log cabin, and gradually Hearthstone Harbor grew and grew. They added more buildings. There was another rustic cabin in the area which was moved and renovated to become one of the resort cottages. Later still, as Hearthstone Harbor became a destination, Alexander Tremble built a community store in the center of the resort, so now people could stay all summer long and pick up supplies as they needed them in the store. They could come for the summer and never leave. It was paradise."

"It sounds like it," Scott said.

"And to think that it all started with the single log cabin! Bill said. Well, it continued to grow, both in size and popularity, all through the 1900s, and even survived several weather disasters along the way, to become one of the best summer resorts on the East Coast. Amazing, isn't it?"

"And it still exists today?" Scott said.

Bill nodded and looked again over the wildlands. He paused for a moment, gathering his thoughts.

"This is where the story comes around to where we are today," he said. "This is the part that I want to share with you. You see, over time, that resort was passed down from generation to generation. We don't live forever, Scott."

"I am coming to realize this," Scott said.

Bill nodded. "The older I get, the less I am able to fool myself, too."

"So, what happened to the resort?"

"Oh, it is still there. But with each generation, it was split among the children, and their children, and so on down the line, until now here we are in the 5th generation of Alexander Tremble and the resort has been split so many times that the family didn't know what to do with it. Here you have what began as a single-family vacation home, becoming a large corporation, surviving not only natural disasters but no fewer than 7 significant tax law changes along the way. All that history, all those memories. What do you do?"

Bill looked up at Scott.

"What would you do, Scott, if you were faced with that type of decision? They were experiencing many of the same things you are experiencing now, a huge tax burden, the possibility of losing what their family had spent generations building, the desire to hold on and also to look forward toward the future. So, what would you do?"

Scott felt his heartbeat thud in his chest. He felt the old familiar feelings of stress and anxiety begin to rise in his throat. Suddenly, he felt very thirsty.

"I …" he began hoarsely. "I don't know what I would do."

Bill nodded. "With great wealth, with great opportunity, there is always responsibility, isn't there? Why don't they teach us that when we are growing up? We spend so much time accumulating wealth, getting ahead, achieving great success – but what they don't tell you is *what happens when you gain it all?*"

"So … what did they do?" Scott asked.

Bill smiled again. "Good question. Excellent question, in fact. And fortunately, this story has a happy ending. But do you want a glass of water first? I could use one myself."

Scott nodded weakly and Bill excused himself for a moment to go inside and retrieve the water. While he was gone, Scott slowed his breathing and looked up at the night sky. It was dark now, and in the absence of porch lights or streetlamps the sky was filled with thousands of glittering stars. Scott crossed the deck and gently removed the cover from the telescope and pulled away the lens cap. He peered into the eyepiece, trying to adjust the telescope to bring the moon back into focus. In doing so, in the gentle turn of the knobs, standing back to observe the glowing silver orb in the sky and then again into the telescope to focus the lens, he felt himself calm, he felt his breathing become steady and his heart rate slow once again.

Footsteps sounded behind him and then Bill's cheerful voice:

"Careful, you'll find yourself out here every night looking at the stars."

"I'm sorry," Scott said. "I was trying to see the moon again."

Bill laughed. "You can use this any time you want. That's why it's here."

He was carrying two glasses of water and now he handed one to Scott. They stood together on the deck and Bill raised his glass slightly:

> "Though my soul may set in darkness, it will rise in perfect light;
> I have loved the stars too fondly to be fearful of the night."

"What was that?" Scott said.

"Sarah Williams," Bill said. 'The Old Astronomer to His Pupil."

"So, you just have a poem for every occasion?"

Bill laughed. "It certainly seems that way, doesn't it? They say it so much better than I ever could."

He gestured toward the chairs.

"Would you like to hear the rest of the story?"

Scott replaced the lens cap and the telescope cover and then he joined Bill on the wooden easy chairs. They sat together in silence for a few minutes, sipping cool water. For the first time, Scott did not feel that the silence was awkward, that he needed to fill it with sound or lower his head down or feel nervous in any way. He was shocked at what was happening to him, and the way he was beginning to drop his guard with Bill Jones. Who was this man, and what was his angle?

"So," Bill said. "We have gone through the history of Hearthstone Harbor, a beautiful family summer paradise. And through the generations it has been passed down, until now when the original family tree has grown so many lovely branches that they all own a piece of the resort and want to know how to both preserve its legacy and avoid terrible tax penalties that would threaten their own wealth and the future of the place."

He sipped his water and continued.

"There were multiple family meetings where everyone was trying to decide what to do. Some were concerned that environmental changes like global warming would make a concentrated asset like a beachside resort enormously susceptible to risk, so as an investment property it did not make sense. But others relied on income from the resort, which was still running well and generating revenue. So, what was happening was that some of the family members were selling off cottages, piecemeal, with others holding onto their property, and because of this the investment was losing value over time. You take that and combine it with onerous tax laws, and they were looking at the real possibility that a third or more of their inheritance would be wiped out just on tax penalties alone."

"That's terrible," Scott said. "So, what did they do? Did they sell the whole property?"

"That was an option," Bill said. "Of course, there were several problems with that. First, the offers that were coming in were insultingly low. Mostly made by developers who first thing would raze the buildings – they saw more value in the land than the resort. So, if they decided to sell all of Hearthstone Harbor at the amounts being offered by developers, they would lose about half of their asset value."

Scott started to feel his stress levels rise again.

"This is exactly what I am afraid of," he said. "You work so hard to build something, and then in a moment you lose it all."

"Exactly," Bill said. "But these family members are smart, and they were all working together to figure out the best outcome. They didn't want to wipe out their assets, clearly, and of course there was the other issue."

"The other issue?"

"Legacy, Scott. The history of the family. Remember that Hearthstone Harbor, one of the most popular resorts along the Maine waterfront, had started with a log cabin in the 1800s. These children had grown up knowing this resort, had grown up hearing the history of their family, as had their parents and their parents before them. Do you want to be the one to wipe out your family's history?"

"Absolutely not," Scott said. "So, selling it off is not an option, and selling it one piece at a time was slowly killing off their assets – gaining in the short term but losing big in the long term. So, what did they do?"

Bill smiled.

"Do you study math much, Scott?"

"Not as a subject, no. Not since college."

"The thing about math is that you are not just looking for the right solution to the problem. That is, of course, the primary concern. You want the solution to work. And there are so many solutions that just don't work, so you keep working the problem and working the problem from all different angles. And suddenly, you arrive at the answer."

"So?"

"So, it is not just the right solution that you are after, Scott. You want the most *elegant* solution."

"What are you trying to tell me, Bill?"

"I am telling you that this family came up with not only the right solution, but the most elegant one, too. A beautiful solution."

"I swear, Bill – if you start with another poem ..."

Bill laughed.

"Not this time. Although there are a few that would easily apply!"

He took another drink of his water and set the glass down, then leaned forward in his chair, clearly excited about the news he wanted to share.

"They were dealing really with three aspects of the problem: How to allow family members to keep their property if they wanted to, how to give other family members the mechanism to sell their property without decreasing the value or facing tax burdens, and how to preserve the family history and legacy."

He smiled again, broader this time. His green eyes flashed.

"And they did it."

"How?" Scott said.

"By giving it away," Bill said. "Or more specifically, by reinvesting it as a charitable trust. Doing well by doing good."

"I don't understand that," Scott said. "How is that possible?"

"They set up a charitable trust for each family. And the property became assets in that charitable trust via corporate stock. For families that want to sell, as they sell their property, that is distributed again into the trust. Because the charitable trust is a *tax-free entity*, they are paying zero tax on the sale of their assets. Not only that, but they produce more capital for future generations – meaning their children and grandchildren will be secured in the future and they can reinvest some of that income as insurance to replace the asset value."

"But I still don't understand," Scott said. "How will this solve all three problems at once?"

"Alexander Tremble was a visionary," Bill said. "He knew how to plan for the future, and he was often way ahead of his time. Do you remember that he built a country store to serve residents when they came for the summer?"

"Yes," Scott said.

"And that country store became the center of all the activity in the resort? It was the centerpiece, the hub of the entire enterprise."

"I remember."

"Well, they created a charitable trust in concert with a small foundation, and they are turning that country store into not only the centerpiece of the resort but a family history and legacy museum. It can be run as a non-profit, educating visitors every summer about the legacy of Alexander Tremble and the generations that followed. Some family members can sell their property without worrying about creating a burden for the rest of the family, and others can hold onto their real estate and enjoy the continued rental income."

"They were able to do all of that?"

"An elegant solution, and the best solution," Bill said. "And you know what else?"

"What?"

"It's going to save them over 8 million dollars."

Scotts' mouth fell open before he was aware of what was happening, and Bill sat back in his chair and laughed.

"That was my reaction when I first heard it, too!"

"I don't believe it," Scott said. "It sounds too easy, too perfect …"

"Too elegant?"

"Yes!"

"That is the beauty of charitable giving," Bill said. "You can help others and help yourself at the same time. Not every day you can come up with a win-win-win scenario … but there it is."

Scott shook his head, still unable to believe what he was hearing. There were footsteps on the deck and he turned to see Carol and Martha walking out together, smiling. Carol looked at Scott and raised her eyebrows.

"You boys have been out here half the night! What are you talking about?"

"Oh, all sorts of things," Bill said. "Stars, math, poetry, history. Right, Scott?"

Scott shook his head again.

"Right," he said. "All sorts of things."

"Well, we should be getting home soon," Carol said. "If you're ready to call it a night, Scott."

"Yes," Scott said, standing. "Yes, I should be going."

As he stood though, a thought suddenly occurred to him.

"I don't understand," he said to Bill. "This sounds all well and good for your friends, but I am not dealing with generations of wealth here. How is this supposed to help me?"

Bill laughed.

"I have something for you."

He disappeared into the house and returned with a book. He handed it to Scott.

"Ben Franklin?" Scott said.

"Come back next weekend," Bill said. "We'll talk some more."

To his wife's surprise, Scott agreed.

Bill and Martha walked Carol and Scott to the entry way and bid them good night. They walked out into the cool evening, turned down the sidewalk that was still aglow from the lights of Jones Manor, and made their way home.

Inside the house, Carol turned to him with a smile.

"What?" Scott said.

"Could it be?" Carol said. "Are you becoming friends with Bill Jones?"

"Let's not get ahead of ourselves," Scott said.

A Note from the Author

Property ownership holds significant value as an asset that can be strategically leveraged through the establishment of a charitable trust. In the case of Hearthstone Harbor, the decision to create individual charitable trusts for each family member emerged as the optimal solution. Not only did this approach alleviate the burden of excessive tax liabilities, but it also bestowed them with the power to shape the future of their philanthropic endeavors.

A remarkable advantage arises for any family member who chooses to sell their property from Hearthstone Harbor. By reinvesting the proceeds into the established charitable trust, they effectively sidestep the tax obligations typically associated with property sales. This intelligent reinvestment strategy preserves their hard-earned wealth while simultaneously benefiting their chosen charitable causes.

Moreover, the creation of a family foundation imparts a sense of permanence and ensures the property's enduring legacy for future generations. This transformative structure tackles both immediate concerns, such as the management of separate properties, and long-term aspirations, such as preserving the cherished family heritage. By consolidating their assets within a family foundation, the family achieves a harmonious alignment between their present needs and their vision for the future.

By harnessing the potential of property ownership through charitable trusts, the family of Hearthstone Harbor not only secures their financial well-being but also leaves a lasting impact on the causes they hold dear. This strategic approach empowers them to overcome immediate challenges while safeguarding their family's enduring legacy, thus creating a legacy that transcends mere property ownership.

Discussion Questions

1. How much wealth is 'enough' for you?

2. What are the three most important things you hope to accomplish with your wealth?

    a.

    b.

    c.

For more information on donating property into a charitable trust, visit www.IncreaseYourWorth.org.

CHAPTER 3

The next week was a blur. Scott worked hard at New Wave Technologies, but if he was being honest with himself, his mind was not really there. He kept turning over and over in his mind the thoughts of Hearthstone Harbor and the family that found a way to preserve their family legacy and provide for future generations. The thoughts kept him up at night still.

In the darkness he would rise with his heart thudding in his chest, and he would sit on the edge of the bed and look out through the soft curtains to the night sky, the silhouette of Jones Manor, and above that, the glimmer of the moon.

All week he would rise in the dark and go through the same routine, letting his heart beat slow down, letting his breathing ease, walking the hallway like a ghost, checking on his girls to make sure they were sleeping and safe, then toward the back door and out on the deck, sitting alone with his thoughts and the sounds of the natural world, slipping into the peace of all the wildness that existed just below his home. He would breathe deeply the night air and calm himself, wait until he was in control of his anxiety, and then he would go inside.

An easy chair and beside that, a table, and a short lamp. He would click on the light. Resting on the table was a copy of the Ben Franklin book that Bill had given him. He would open to his bookmarked page and begin reading.

From time to time, he would stop and dwell on certain sentences, descriptions of the life and philosophy of Franklin:

> *History is a tale, Franklin came to believe, not of immutable forces but of human endeavors.*

After the first night he began keeping a stack of index cards and an ink pen beside his book on the table, and when he reached a passage of particular interest, he would write it down:

> *While gambling at checkers with some shipmates, he formulated an 'infallible rule,' which was that 'if two persons equal in judgment play for a considerable sum, he that loves money most shall lose, his anxiety for the success of the game confounds him.'*

He set the book down then and simply read the passage that he had written on the index card, repeating the words like a mantra, and then settling back in his easy chair and closing his eyes, turning the words over and over again in his mind. He knew which of the 'two persons equal in judgment' he was in this scenario and knew that his anxiety would cause him to lose everything.

But how could he ease that burden? How could he do what Bill Jones was asking him to do, which seemed to run so counter to what he had been taught his entire life? You were supposed to accumulate wealth through hard work and diligence, intelligence, sometimes through guile – though never through treachery – and then you were supposed to keep your wealth, grow it, secure a place for your children and their children, so that their lives would be made easier because of your efforts. He felt as though he were on the verge of succeeding in all those important ways, but that he was also one misstep away from losing it all.

He continued reading and located another passage worthy of an index card. Carefully he wrote down the words in his close, small handwriting:

> *Through his self-improvement tips for cultivating personal virtues and his civic-improvement schemes for furthering the common good, he helped to create, and to celebrate, a new ruling class of ordinary citizens.*

This seemed to be more in line with what Bill Jones was saying, especially 'his civic-improvement schemes for furthering the common good.' There must be a way to use wealth to improve your own standing as well as the standing of those around you – both your loved ones and the community at large. But how?

Scott did not own a beach resort. He was not being asked to reinvest generations of assets into a charitable trust. As a matter of fact, he was still unsure of what exactly he was being asked to do. The more he considered this, the more he realized that Bill Jones had never specifically asked him to do *anything*. He merely told him a story about some friends of his and their incredible Maine beach resort.

But how could Scott have a story like that? He was only one person, and he didn't know what he wanted to do to 'further the common good.' He knew only that he wanted his family to be safe, his daughters to have bright futures, and for him to not have to *worry* so much every day of his life, the way he was doing now.

For years, his whole life really, Scott had been working toward goals he thought were worthwhile:

Earn a living that will provide for yourself and your family.

Strive to be your best every day.

Always reach for that next achievement that is just beyond your grasp. Stay hungry. Stay ambitious.

Never forget the people who helped you when you needed it most.

He had followed those goals from the day he started at New Wave Technologies, a young kid with no idea where his life was going to take him. And each day, each year of his life, he had risen through the ranks of the company, he had achieved every goal that he had set out to reach. He had a beautiful family, a good home, and he had *earned* it all through his own hard work and dedication. And now, right when he was poised to gain everything that he had worked so hard for, it was slipping out of his grasp.

And then, he found another stirring passage:

> *Those who met with greater economic success in life were responsible to help those in genuine need …*

The line struck him like a thunderbolt. It was as though Benjamin Franklin himself were speaking to him in that moment, telling him exactly what his responsibility was. It was the voice of Ben Franklin and Bill Jones coming together to counsel Scott in his decision, reminding him that he was responsible 'to help those in genuine need.'

If only I knew how to do that, Scott said to the empty room. His eyes were tired and he closed them, his vision a soft orange in the glow of the lamp light. He slipped the index card into the book and turned off the light, and then he allowed himself to drift into a fitful and troubled sleep.

At last, Saturday morning arrived. Carol and the girls were going to be in the city running errands and enjoying the day together, and Scott was free to spend his time at Jones Manor. It was a beautiful blue-sky spring morning, the air was fresh, the trees were bright green across the land, and birds circled the air and called to each other in their boisterous and energetic songs.

Bill met Scott at the door and without any hesitation led him toward the backyard, where they took up their positions on the wooden deck chairs. He had already set out two glasses of water and an ice pitcher on a table between them, and the glasses were cold and sweating small beads of cool water down the sides. Scott lifted his and held it up toward Bill.

"To furthering the common good," he said.

Bill smiled knowingly and they both took a refreshing drink of water. Setting down their glasses, Bill said, "You have been enjoying the book, I see."

"He was an incredible man," Scott said. "He accomplished more in his lifetime than I could ever dream of."

"You have a long way to go," Bill said. "You may surprise yourself and surpass even the great Benjamin Franklin."

"If I can accomplish even a tenth of what he did, I will be happy."

"As he said and I have shamelessly repeated, wealth comes with responsibility," Bill said. "One of those responsibilities is to help those who are in need, to further the common good, as you so eloquently put it."

"That is what I am trying to do," Scott said. "But how do I do it? I have been going around and around with this question, and I can never seem to arrive at a satisfying answer."

"An elegant solution," Bill said.

"Exactly."

Bill nodded and looked out over the wildland. He took a long drink of water before placing his glass carefully onto the table.

"It might help to know what you are passionate about," Bill said. "Who do you want to help?"

Scott considered the question for a moment and then shook his head.

"I am not sure. Until these recent weeks, I haven't given that much thought."

Bill nodded again thoughtfully.

"Do you have time for another story?" He asked.

"More friends of yours?"

Bill laughed.

"What can I say? I love people."

*

"I have a friend named George Connors," Bill said. "He reminds me a bit of you, in fact."

"Why is that?" Scott said.

"Well, you are both smart, successful, built something from your own hard work and determination, were not born into wealth but created it on your own."

Scott tried not to smile at the compliments and nodded along while Bill continued.

"He and his wife, Rose, worked very hard over their lifetimes to accumulate their financial freedom, and they were both earning enough to afford them a comfortable lifestyle as well as the ability to make annual donations to different charities. Much like you and Carol have done in your own lives."

"Yes," Scott offered. "We make our contributions to groups that we are passionate about, and the girls help us make year-end donations. But we are not talking about modest annual giving, Bill. This is a huge amount of money."

Bill lifted his hand in a friendly way.

"Of course," he said, smiling. "George and Rose were in that position exactly. George was heavily involved in their local church, and they would donate around 50 thousand a year to help with the general fund and to support special projects. They were generous with their time and money, but as you say, in the big picture these were modest contributions. Difference makers, without a doubt, but not exactly in line with what you are trying to accomplish."

"Is that it?" Scott said. "Is that the story?"

Bill laughed.

"Scott," he said. "I know we have not spent a lot of time together, but I think you know by now that I take a while to tell the complete story."

"Well, that is true," Scott said.

"I want you to see the whole picture," Bill said. "So, if you will please indulge me?"

"Go ahead," Scott said. "I will try not to interrupt."

"Thank you," Bill said. He took a drink of water and looked out over the back fence.

"Boy, it sure is beautiful out here, isn't it," he said. "Isn't this wonderful, to sit out here on a glorious day and hear the sounds of nature all around us?"

Scott stopped for a moment, listening. When he allowed himself to settle back and focus on the different sounds, they began to come to him. The creek water running fast over the rocks, the trees swaying in a light *swish,* birds calling out in different voices, a bluebird with its harsh screech, the red-breasted house finch singing its lyrical song. Scott closed his eyes and felt the cool breeze on his face, the warmth of the sunshine.

"I am so thankful to have this space out here," Bill said, his voice low and soft, as though he were trying hard to not interrupt the natural sounds.

Scott opened his eyes.

"I think you are getting sidetracked again," he said.

Bill smiled.

"Yes, sorry. Martha will tell you that it is one of my most maddening habits. So, where was I?"

"George and the church."

"Right, thank you. George would make annual contributions to his local church, but Rose – well, she was a bit more like me, she loved animals and wanted to do whatever she could to ensure they were protected and well cared for. It can be difficult to protect them when developers are consistently overrunning their habitats, when they are being overhunted, when people do not care for their own pets and turn them loose without any hope for survival."

Bill shook his head as though to free himself from those bad images.

"As I was saying, Rose loves animals and would do anything for them. So, she made her annual contributions to local animal shelters as well as to a wildlife reserve that was located near their home. Just like George, her giving was modest and consistent, important. She wanted to make a difference and this was how she wanted to do it."

"It sounds like they were both doing good work in their community," Scott said.

"Oh, they were! Like so many people, they were making their mark where they could. But they always wanted to do more. Again, like most people. If you are in a position to help someone, wouldn't you do that?"

"Those who meet with greater economic success in life are responsible to help those in genuine need," Scott said.

"Exactly," Bill said. "And suddenly, they would find themselves – much like you – in a position to do exactly that."

"What happened?" Scott asked.

"Well, one of their companies went public," Bill said. "Suddenly, the company stock options they were holding were now worth about $2 million in ordinary income. Just like that, Scott."

"A life-changing moment," Scott said.

"But now they were facing a dilemma. What should they do with their sudden windfall? You know as well as anyone that if they were to simply hold onto it, they would end up paying a significant amount in taxes. They would lose their opportunity to create meaningful change in the world, to establish their legacy, to possibly create something that would last well beyond their own lives."

"So, what did they do?" Scott said. "Give it away?"

Bill smiled. "You're starting to catch on now, Scott."

"Thank you," Scott said reluctantly.

"George and Rose were committed to giving back to their communities in various ways. We have already established that they made annual contributions of approximately $50 thousand to their local church, and another $50 thousand to the local animal shelters and wildlife reserve. Good, consistent donations."

"So?"

"So, if you are already committed to doing that – if you know that you will make these donations every year for the rest of your lives … why not do it all upfront?"

"All upfront?" Scott said. "I don't understand what you mean by that."

"George and Rose set up what is called a charitable lead trust. Essentially, what they did was take the next 20 years of charitable donations and give it all at once. Instead of tens of thousands of dollars, we are now talking about millions of dollars for their favorite charities."

"You can do that?" Scott asked.

"Absolutely you can!" Bill said. "And what makes the charitable lead trust such a compelling option is that you immediately gain the tax deduction for your donation. Instead of losing significant wealth to tax penalties, you save with tax deductions."

"Wow," Scott said.

"Listen," Bill said. "It's not the tax that's the problem. We all pay taxes. The problem is that you don't have any power over your own wealth. You have worked for decades – it is *your work* – and now you want to decide what to do with it. You don't want to just hand it over to Uncle Sam, where it will disappear and you will never see it again."

"That's what I am afraid will happen," Scott said. "It will just disappear."

"That is not the way you change your community," Bill said. "You can't give all your hard-earned wealth to the federal government and then expect that they will support your local church. Or save wild animals. Or any other project you think is significant and necessary. They don't live here, Scott. You do. And now you have the power to do something about it, right now, using what you have worked so hard to earn."

Bill continued.

"The best part of this is that your wealth is now being directed where *you want it to go*. George and Rose were in complete control of their charitable giving. They were able to direct their money to support the causes they were most passionate about. They did well by doing good."

"It seems really simple when you explain it this way," Scott said. "Almost too easy."

"We only believe that difficult problems require complex solutions," Bill said. "But I prefer the words of Niklaus Wirth."

"Niklaus Wirth?"

"Swiss computer scientist?" Bill said. "Creator of PASCAL?"

Scott shook his head. "I have no idea what you are talking about."

Bill shrugged and then looked out into the distance and spoke from memory:

"Complexity has and will maintain a strong fascination for many people. It is true that we live in a complex world and strive to solve inherently complex problems, which often do require complex mechanisms. However, this should not diminish our desire for elegant solutions which convince by their clarity and effectiveness."

He paused for a moment, as though for emphasis, to allow the words to settle on the air. Then he continued:

"Simple, elegant solutions are more effective, but they are harder to find than complex ones, and they require more time, which we too often believe to be unaffordable."

"So," Bill said. "Take some time. Find the elegant solution. It is possible."

"I guess I need to decide what I really care about," Scott said.

Bill did not answer right away. He was focused on the sights and sounds below in the wilderness. The birds circling in the sky. Finally, he turned toward Scott again. But this time, there was something slightly different about him, like he was coming back after being in a dream.

"Everything okay?" Scott asked.

Bill smiled. He shook his head and smiled again, fully returning to the present moment.

"Wonderful," he said.

*

Later that evening, long after Scott had left Bill's house and come home, Carol and the girls returned from their day in the city. Scott invited them out onto the back deck, where he had set up food and drinks. The sun was setting in the distance, a beautiful rich glow of red, pink, and purple. Shadows stretched across the lawn.

"What's the occasion?" Carol asked. The girls happily sat in deck chairs and helped themselves to the plates of food and the drinks.

"We never sit out here," Scott said. "We are always too busy. Or I am, anyway. I thought it would be nice to spend an evening together as a family."

Carol smiled and let her hand rest on Scott's shoulder for a moment.

"I think that is a wonderful idea," she said. "What do you think, girls?"

Emily nodded while chewing her food and Savannah looked up from her plate.

"Have you figured out what you're going to do with all that money yet?"

Scott laughed.

"You don't waste any time, do you?"

"What?" Savannah said, giving an exaggerated shrug. "I'm just wondering!"

Carol sat beside Scott and helped herself to the food and drinks. Soon they were eating together in the quiet of the backyard, while the sun set gently over the west like a slowing closing eye.

After a while, Scott set his plate to the side and sat up to face his family.

"I was hoping that maybe you girls could help decide what we do with it," he said.

"Really?" Savannah said, bolting upright. "We should spend it! Buy a new house, maybe travel, first-class of course, or a private jet ..."

"Savannah, please!" Emily said. "We are not going to waste it like that. Dad knows what he is doing and we are not going to be greedy with what we have. Besides, we have enough already, and I like this house."

Savannah settled back in her chair and crossed her arms.

"It was just *an idea*, Em," she said. "I never said we *had to do it*."

"Well, it is selfish," Emily said. "Besides, Dad wants to further the common good, right Dad? It's our responsibility to help those in genuine need?"

"Where did you learn that?" Scott asked.

Emily grinned sheepishly. "I may have seen the notecards in your Benjamin Franklin book."

"Well, you are right about that," Scott said. "And Savannah, we will always have enough to support the things that we want to do – although I don't know about a private jet. But if we keep it, we'll lose a significant amount to taxes."

"Why would that happen?" Savannah said.

"See, this is what they should be teaching us in school," Emily said. "We never learn about how money actually works, and how to build for the future, and taxes, and the things that really matter when you are growing up. All we learn about is algebra and maybe a little bit of history and, I don't know, poetry."

"Well, learning poetry isn't all that bad," Scott said.

Carol turned to him with her eyebrows raised.

"Really?" She said, smiling. "Who are you, and what have you done with my husband?"

"I'm just saying, poetry can be useful in certain situations."

Carol shook her head and smiled again.

"So, what do you need help with?" Emily asked.

"Well, I have been thinking that one of the best ways to preserve our way of life and help others at the same time is to set up some sort of charitable trust."

"Like, for charities?" Savannah asked.

"Yes, it could be used for just about anything that promotes the public good," Scott explained.

"Which charity are we going to support?" Savannah asked.

"That is the problem, right there," Scott said. "I have no idea where I want to direct our funds. I keep hearing stories about how other people have set up trusts and foundations to do really great work, like saving their family beach resort or supporting churches and animal shelters – things they really care about."

"And?"

"And I can't think of something I care about that much."

Scott stared off into the distance.

"I guess I just don't want to make a mistake."

There was silence then. He had never said that aloud to his family before, and for a moment they all sat together, peering out into the growing darkness.

Finally, Emily spoke up.

"Dad," she said. "We'll think of something great. Savannah and I will come up with some ideas, won't we Savannah?"

"Definitely!" Savannah said. "And I promise, none of them will be a private jet!"

Scott chuckled softly. "Thank you, girls. That means a lot."

They spent the rest of that evening watching the last of the sunset and finishing their meals, and then the girls gathered the plates and glasses and took them inside and washed them. They did not return to the backyard after that but instead went down the hall to Emily's room, where soon the sound of music could be heard drifting out from behind the closed door.

Scott and Carol stayed together in the darkness of the backyard. The sky was now a beautiful deep blue and black.

"It is really lovely out here," Carol said. "Thank you for doing this."

"You're welcome," Scott said. "I suppose I never noticed it quite like this before."

"Sounds like Bill is having a positive effect on you."

"I'm not sold yet, but I have to admit – I didn't hate being over there today."

"Well, that's good," Carol said. "Because they want us to join them for a dinner party next weekend."

Scott sighed and refilled his water glass with the ice pitcher.

"I'm not sure I like them that much," Scott said. "But all right, I'll go."

A Note from the Author

The power of strategic charitable giving goes beyond regular donations with the establishment of charitable trusts. Take inspiration from the story of George and Rose, whose wise decision to utilize a charitable lead trust yielded remarkable benefits, including substantial tax deductions.

Traditionally, donors contribute a set amount each year to their preferred charitable organizations. However, George and Rose took a different approach by creating charitable lead trusts to support the church and the wildlife sanctuary for a fixed period of 20 years. By front-loading their donations, they ensured that a significant sum of $1 million was allocated to each entity.

The ingenious mechanism of the charitable lead trust operates as follows: Every year, the trust disburses a predetermined amount to both the church and the wildlife sanctuary, allowing them to thrive and fulfill their missions. At the end of the 20-year period, any remaining funds within the trust are either returned to the donor or designated to a chosen recipient or heir.

Through this strategic approach, George and Rose not only demonstrated their unwavering support for their favored causes but also maximized the impact of their philanthropy. By consolidating their donations into charitable lead trusts, they enjoyed the benefits of a significant tax deduction while ensuring a sustained and meaningful contribution over a fixed period.

To fully harness the potential of charitable lead trusts and ensure they align with your unique financial situation and philanthropic goals, it is highly recommended to seek guidance from an experienced financial advisor. By consulting with a trusted expert, you can receive personalized advice and comprehensive insights that will empower you to make informed decisions regarding charitable lead trusts. Together with your advisor, you can navigate the complexities of this strategic giving tool, optimize its benefits, and pave the way for a truly impactful and fulfilling philanthropic journey.

Discussion Questions

1. Do you already support charities with gifts and donations? If so, which charities – and why?

    a.

    b.

    c.

2. When it comes to charitable giving, what are three areas that you are most passionate about?

    a.

    b.

    c.

Want to learn how you can reduce your taxes through charitable lead trusts? Visit www.stickneyresearch.com and view our Tax

Reduction Strategies.

CHAPTER 4

After the great weekend he had with his family, Scott believed that his problems would finally be behind him. He would find the right solution, he and his family would quickly decide on a charitable cause that they were passionate about, and he would be able to move forward with his life – happily.

None of that happened.

The intervening days between the previous weekend and the upcoming dinner party at Jones Manor passed slowly, every ticking minute a reminder that Scott had not yet made a decision. It was not so much that he had not landed on the right charity – although that was certainly part of the problem – but there was a larger issue at play, too.

In the night, when he was alone in the low light of the front room, reading Benjamin Franklin's book or staring into the emptiness, or when he walked out onto the back deck and felt the spring air on his face, he would slowly and inevitably arrive at the same conclusion.

First, that even with the stories that were told to him, even when Bill Jones laid out the charitable giving plan in great detail, Scott still did not fully understand the process. That part made him uneasy, like he was missing something obvious if he could just open his eyes and his mind.

Second, the stories themselves seemed too good to be true. Sure, it could work for generations of families that had over a hundred years of wealth – and yes, there were George and Rose, front-loading 20 years of donations to their favorite charities. But that seemed impossible for Scott. Those ideas made sense for those specific situations, but he still held serious doubts that he could make it work for himself and for his family.

Bill caught him in the middle of the week while he was taking out the trash.

"Glad I ran into you!" Bill said. "Hey, are you feeling alright?"

"It's been a long week and it's only half over," Scott said, straightening the trash cans against the curb.

He paused for a moment with his hand resting against the can lid. It was clear Bill wanted to share something with him.

Scott closed his eyes and breathed for a moment. Bracing himself.

"What's on your mind?"

"Just got off the phone with my friend, Jill. She works at a medical device company – and it's about to go public."

"And?"

"And I think she may have the solution you've been looking for."

Scott paused for a moment, looking down the empty street. The sun had recently set and cool air drifted down from the swaying trees.

"What's the solution, Bill?"

Bill leaned in, his voice lowering as if sharing a secret.

"She's set to receive a boatload of stock options, worth about $20 each. Now, here's the interesting part. She's passionate about a local charity that helps homeless women and children, founded by another tech entrepreneur."

"Okay, so what's Jill doing with these options?" Scott asked.

Bill smiled.

"Well, Jill's looking into creating a partnership with the charity, giving them the non-voting units. She's planning to invest around $19 million of her potential earnings into this partnership, which would allow her to give 90% of it to the charity."

Scott's eyes widened.

"That's a lot of money, Bill. What's in it for Jill?" he asked.

Bill maintained his warm smile.

"It's all about taxes, Scott," he said. "By doing this, Jill can significantly reduce her tax liability. She'd be contributing to the charity, avoiding taxes on the donated amount, and still maintaining control over how the funds are used as the general partner."

"So, she's basically helping the charity and herself at the same time," Scott continued.

"Exactly! It's a win-win," Bill said. "Jill's supporting her favorite charity while minimizing the taxes she'd owe on her substantial windfall. It's a tax-efficient way to make a difference in the community and manage her wealth."

Scott listened, but still there was the nagging feeling in the back of his mind. How could any of this possibly help him? It felt less like an education and more like Bill Jones just loved to talk about his successful friends.

Finally, he stopped Bill.

"I understand what you're trying to tell me – I think," Scott said. "But I don't know if I can achieve the same results, or even how to begin."

"Are you afraid to fail, Scott?" Bill asked.

"I'm afraid to get it wrong," Scott said. "I'm afraid that I will do something wrong and throw away everything I've worked for. That my kids won't have the future I imagined for them."

He paused for a moment.

"I'm afraid of a lot of things, to be honest. I'm not Jill, or George and Rose, or Alexander Tremble. I'm not Ben Franklin. I don't have the type of wealth to get things wrong."

"It's not their wealth that matters," Bill said. "You're focusing on the wrong part of the story."

"And what is the right part?"

"The wealth … that's just a number, Scott. What we're talking about is *impact*. You have a rare opportunity to impact the world around you – to change people's lives, including your own."

Bill paused for a moment, his words hanging in the evening air.

"So," he continued. "What impact do you want to have?"

"I … don't know," Scott said.

Bill smiled.

"You will," he said. "Trust me, you will."

He said goodnight and walked back to his estate, leaving Scott standing on the curb in front of his own house, his hand resting on the garbage can lid. It was some time before he was able to walk back inside.

The nights dragged on and on. It began to take a toll on his work. He was tired all the time. And it seemed as though the harder he tried to solve the problem, the more elusive the answers became. And the only thing more elusive than the right solution was his own sleep. He became a walking ghost, haunting his own home in the night. Even time spent on the back deck could not help him this time.

One night, as he was walking up and down the hallway, he noticed the faint glow of a lamp shining from under Savannah's door. He turned the knob slowly and walked inside, where he found Savannah sitting at her desk, writing in a notebook.

"What are you doing up so late?" He asked quietly.

"Couldn't sleep," Savannah said, not looking up from her book.

"What are you working on?" Scott asked. He stepped into the room and closed the door quietly behind him.

"It all seems so unfair," Savannah said.

"What does?"

"Life," Savannah said. "How some people get chances and other people don't."

Scott sat on the edge of Savannah's bed and stared into the room. Clothes and books were strewn on the floor.

"I just think that it's incredible that because we were born into this family, we automatically have all these chances that other kids don't have," Savannah continued. "Like, I didn't do anything to earn it, it was all random chance."

She paused.

"I don't really want a private jet," she said. "It was just something that popped into my head. I'm sorry I said it."

Scott sighed and rubbed his eyes.

"You are a really thoughtful girl," he said. "And I am glad you are my daughter."

Savannah set her pen down and closed her notebook. She turned around.

"What are we going to *do,* Dad? How can we help kids who don't have the same chances I have?"

Her eyes blazed with hope and passion.

"I mean, I know that it's impossible to give everyone the same thing – but just an opportunity to make something for themselves. Like, if everyone could go to a good school, if they have a chance to learn. Even just having a good home, or being safe, food on the table every day …"

She opened her notebook and scanned the contents.

"… I don't know, I have a lot of ideas."

Scott smiled and stood. He crossed the room and kissed Savannah on the top of her head.

"I love your ideas," he said.

"Do you really think we can help people?"

"I do," Scott said. He did not say anything else, did not say that he didn't know how to accomplish that goal.

"Time for sleep," he said. He walked to the door and stood just inside for a moment.

"Dad?" Savannah said.

"Yes?"

"You should get some sleep, too."

Scott stepped into the hallway and closed the door. After a moment, the glow beneath the door switched off. He stood alone in the darkness. Something Savannah said resonated in his mind.

It's impossible to give everyone the same thing – but just an opportunity to make something for themselves.

Perhaps that was a start. Scott considered it for a moment, but he couldn't generate a single concrete idea. It was as though the best idea was right there in front of him, if only he could grasp it. Yet he couldn't.

Everyone had ideas. And with each passing day, Scott realized that he was getting no closer to making a decision. Soon the expiration date would arrive. He was running out of time.

And so, the week proceeded in this way, and without realizing it he looked up from his office desk to find that it was Friday, and time to go home for another weekend.

The dinner party was that Saturday night. He and Carol left the house and walked the short distance down the sidewalk to Jones Manor, which was glowing with festive lights. From inside came the sounds of happy voices and when Martha greeted them at the door, laughter could be heard ringing out in the dining room.

"Scott and Carol!" Martha said, smiling brilliantly. "We are so happy you could join us! Please do come in."

Her smile faltered for just a fraction of an instant when her eyes fell upon Scott, and he knew that his own face showed the stress and the sleepless nights.

He followed his wife and Martha as they walked through the house and into the dining room, where Bill was talking to another couple. When Scott and Carol entered the room, he motioned toward them in a friendly way.

"Scott and Carol, it is my pleasure to introduce Joyce and Stuart Peterson, friends of ours from … how long has it been, Stu?"

Stuart was smartly dressed in blue slacks and a white shirt

unbuttoned at the collar, his silver hair cut close and brushed to one side.

"Has to have been 30 … 40 years?" He said.

Joyce stood beside him, matching well in a blue dress, but what really stood out about her was the fact that every piece of jewelry she wore was diamond –two diamond rings, a dazzling bright diamond tennis bracelet, sparkling diamond earrings and a diamond pendant around her neck.

While Martha and Carol spoke with Joyce and Stuart, Bill came across the room and pulled Scott to one side.

"I hate to say it," he said, "but you don't look so great. Everything all right with you?"

Without meaning to, Scott found himself confiding in Bill like an old friend.

"Trouble sleeping," he said.

"Still?"

"It's this decision, it is really weighing on my mind."

"Have you thought about what you are passionate about? Are you still reading the book? What is keeping you up at night?"

The questions came so quickly that Scott could not keep them straight, and in his tired mind he could not formulate answers fast enough.

"I am," he began, but then he paused. He shook his head and rubbed his eyes with the heels of his hands. He shook his head again.

"I can't seem to make any decisions these days," he said. "There is so much pressure riding on my decision that I can't figure out what to do."

"They don't teach us this growing up, do they?"

"Don't teach us what?"

Bill smiled in a sympathetic way.

"Growing up, you think that if you can just make enough, that if you work hard and save your money, that all your problems will be taken care of. See, for most people the primary concern is earning enough income to live, then enough to do the things you really want to do, then to be comfortable, then to leave something behind for your children and your family. It never ends, really."

"I don't understand," Scott said.

"We come to believe that with enough wealth, our problems will just go away," Bill said. "But it doesn't quite work that way. Nobody tells you that once you gain a significant amount of wealth, you are left with more decisions – and problems that you were never taught how to solve. See, you have a rare opportunity to do something great. But that comes with a lot of pressure, too."

"It really does," Scott said. "I can't tell you how much pressure I have been under recently, trying to figure out the best path to take. I keep thinking about the stories that you told me, and then I read the book that you lent to me, but I can't quite figure out how that all applies to my life."

"Well, maybe tonight will be helpful to you then," Bill said.

"Why is that?" Scott asked.

But before he could have that question answered, Martha announced that it was time for the dinner to be served and invited the guests to the table. They sat together around the beautiful dining table and were served vegetable biryani, a delicious dish featuring chickpeas, roasted beets, sweet potatoes, and paneer, topped with a creamy citrus coconut and cilantro sauce. It was one of the best meals Scott had eaten, and for a brief window of time he forgot about his problems and simply enjoyed the elegance of the meal.

He was so involved in his meal that he failed to follow the conversation that was happening around him. It wasn't that he was trying to be rude, only that he had been having difficulty focusing lately and was content in that moment to allow the others to talk at their leisure.

Which was why he was startled when he suddenly heard his name being mentioned. He did not know what they were talking about at the time, but through the fog of his mind came his name, then his name again.

He looked up and listened as Bill gestured down the table toward him.

"Scott has been dealing with it for some time now, and he has to make a decision here in the next few months. It has been a challenging situation, all around – as I am sure you can imagine."

Stuart and Joyce nodded their heads thoughtfully and now and then looked down the table to where Scott was sitting. He looked over to Carol for help but she was listening to Bill speak.

"Scott, you can probably talk about this better than I can," Bill said. "Here I am, monopolizing the conversation!"

"Excuse me?" Scott said.

"Bill was telling them about our decision," Carol said. "About what we plan to do?"

"What we plan to do," Scott repeated. It was as though he could not make his mind catch up with what was being discussed.

Bill helped him along.

"I was just telling Stuart and Joyce here that we have been discussing different options for charitable giving. You know, in relation to what you are going through right now."

Finally, the words clicked into place for Scott. He managed a weak smile.

"I don't think they want to hear about our problems all night," he said.

"Oh, no!" Joyce responded. "We just went through this ourselves in the last two years and would love to hear what you are planning to do."

"You did?" Scott asked. He looked toward Bill and saw that there was a sparkle in his eye. A little smile. He had planned the whole thing.

Scott shook his head and sighed.

"Okay," he said to Joyce and Stuart, "what did you do?"

"Well," Stuart began, "we both have worked for years at Microsoft."

"It's where we met," Joyce said.

"And because we have been there for so many years, we have significant stock awards that are vesting every year," Stuart continued. "We have around $700,000 of income per year that comes from stock awards."

"When you combine that with our salaries, we are looking at well over a million dollars coming in each year," Joyce said.

Scott was impressed, not only by the amount that they were earning but by how finely tuned they were in telling the story. It was clear that they had told this before.

"Our other financial advisors had no real suggestions for what to do with what had quickly become significant wealth," Joyce explained. "We were worried that if we didn't do something fast, we were going to be hit with these incredible taxes and lose a lot of what we gained."

"That is when we learned how to use a charitable remainder trust," Stuart continued. "And you could say it changed everything for us."

"We make contributions every year to the charitable remainder trust," Joyce said, "and by doing that we can avoid a significant amount of tax on those stock grants. The great thing about this type of trust is that we have a reliable retirement income coming out of it every year for as long as we live."

"And we have adult children," Stuart said. "Two boys. At the end of the life of this trust, we can purchase insurance to replace the asset and leave that to our children, so they are still receiving their inheritance."

"It allows us to do what we want now, to pursue our philanthropic goals while we have the chance, and to make sure our boys are taken care of when we die," Joyce said.

"So, everybody wins," Scott said.

"Exactly!" Joyce said. "We have more power in where our money is directed, which is what we always wanted."

"We didn't know much about it at first," Stuart said. "But once we learned, it became the obvious choice for what we were trying to accomplish. It was one of the best decisions we ever made."

"Really?" Scott asked.

"Absolutely," Joyce responded.

"Aside from the clear benefits of managing our finances as we grow older, it gives us the opportunity to make a real difference in the world."

"What difference is that?" Scott asked.

Joyce smiled broadly.

"We support a group that provides clean drinking water to villages throughout the African continent. Something that we take for granted is not always available to every person. And with drought conditions worsening it seems every year, some people have to walk 20-30 miles each day to access drinking water."

"Either that, or they drink contaminated water and expose themselves and their children to terrible diseases," Stuart said.

"With our support," Joyce continued, "they design and build water wells and pumps that secure clean, safe drinking water – right there in the village."

"We regularly receive updates when they build new wells," Stuart said. "It never gets old, knowing that you are making a difference. We made a decision many years ago that if we had the opportunity to positive influence the lives of others, we would take it."

"This has been our opportunity," Joyce concluded.

Scott was struck by their enthusiasm. Like Bill, they seemed to carry themselves more lightly, as though they were not burdened by the weight of living. For them, life seemed to be a place of endless possibilities, and they were doing everything within their power to extend those possibilities to others. Scott found himself wishing that he could feel that way, and he wondered if it was possible. He could not remember the last time that he had not felt under pressure. He wondered what it felt like to be free, like Stuart and Joyce.

"I am curious about something," Carol said.

"What's that?" Joyce asked.

"We have been talking about making a difference on a rather large scale. But what about people who are just getting started, or who maybe don't have the wealth to set up significant trusts like yours?"

"You know," Bill said. "Martha and I have been having that same discussion lately. We are always looking for new opportunities to make an impact, no matter the size."

Martha smiled as she entered the conversation.

"We recently learned about U.S. Legacy Income Trusts. They accomplish a lot of what you are describing, Carol."

"How does it work?" Carol asked.

"It is pretty simple," Martha explained. "And there are some advantages to this strategy if you are just starting out or have a lower financial threshold. Essentially, they are donor-advised funds, and you can choose up to ten charities to support."

Carol's eyes widened. "That certain gives you a lot of options."

"Exactly," Martha said. "You receive a federal income tax deduction, and even more than that, you can designate up to ten individual beneficiaries to receive tax-advantaged income from the trust."

She paused for a moment.

"And that lasts for life," she said. "So, if you have children or loved ones that you want to support, that is an option for you. When the last income beneficiary dies, the remaining funds are passed onto the charities that you designated."

"It has many benefits and a low cost of entry," Bill added. "Which makes it a very intriguing option."

"In fact," Martha continued, "we have a few friends who have started making a difference with Legacy Income Trusts. They were over a few weeks ago, telling us about it."

The guests had finished their dinners, so Martha stood and smiled.

"Come," she said. "Let's leave these for now and make the most of our evening."

"Perhaps we should relocate to the backyard?" Bill asked.

"It is his favorite place," Martha said.

"I go there at the end of every day," Bill said. "It is my sanctuary, you might say."

It was a pleasant, cool spring evening, and the dinner guests chatted happily on the outside deck. Martha had strung lights between the house and the back fence, and a soft glow bathed them all now in gold. It was truly a beautiful night.

It seemed that everywhere he turned, someone was talking about a different charitable giving strategy. As he stood on the deck, he could hear two other people, Nicole and Randall, discussing their donor-advised fund.

"It allows us to make charitable contributions to the fund and receive immediate tax benefits," Nicole was telling the other guests. "We can recommend grants to qualified non-profit organizations over time."

"How did you set it up?" Joyce asked.

"It's really simple, you just make a contribution to a sponsoring organization – in our case it was a capital investment, but you can use stock, securities, or other assets – and then the organization manages the fund for you," Nicole said. "Randall and I are in control of where those funds go now, and we just tell them where to direct our contributions through strategic grants."

"It works perfectly for us," Randall continued. "We are just starting out with charitable giving and this gave us the entry into that world. Plus, the tax benefits are incredible."

"We wanted to find some way to make a difference, but we didn't really know how or where to start," Nicole said. "With a donor-advised fund, we leave all the details and administrative tasks to the professionals, so we get to focus on maximizing our impact."

"So, what are you focused on?" Joyce asked.

"Both of us have a history of Alzheimer's and dementia in our families," Randall said. "So, we are committed to supporting Alzheimer's research and treatment."

"It's our dream to see a cure in our lifetime," Nicole added. "And whatever we can do to further that cause, we will do it."

The conversation continued, with Nicole and Randall providing a rich history of their involvement with research institutions, as well as their personal family stories. Gradually, Scott stopped listening and wandered out to the end of the deck by himself. As wonderful as their stories were, Scott could not listen anymore.

He felt increasingly anxious and doubtful. Here was yet another example of someone making smart investments with their wealth, helping the world while they helped themselves and their families, and he was just sitting on it, unable to make a decision. He was paralyzed with indecision, which made him angry and anxious.

While the other guests engaged in conversation, Scott separated himself from the group and stood near the edge of the yard, looking out over the wildland. Beyond the reach of their voices, he could hear down below the sound of running water. He closed his eyes and breathed in the sweet smell of the trees and the fresh air.

"You can do this," he said to himself. "Focus on your breathing. See what you want in life. Then execute that vision."

It was not entirely different from how he had achieved everything else in his life. He reminded himself that he had started with nothing, that he had worked hard his entire life to get to where he was now. What he had accomplished already was impressive, and it came about because he had a clear focus on what he wanted out of life.

He had not been satisfied settling for 'good enough.' He had always wanted to live an extraordinary life, and he had put all his effort into making that possible. When he was first hired at New Wave Technologies, they were only a small startup, but Scott had seen the possibilities long before anyone else could, he had seen the potential not only to do great work in a field he enjoyed but to gain unprecedented wealth. He had accepted stock options in place of a larger salary at a more established firm because he had seen the potential, and then he had worked every day of his life to realize that potential.

"You can do this," he said to himself again. This time, with a little more conviction. He breathed deeply the night air and listened to the sounds of the trees and the soft wind blowing.

After a while, he sensed someone beside him. He turned to find Bill standing there, staring out into the open space.

"I'm sorry for the ambush," Bill said, still looking straight ahead into the wilderness. "I thought their story might be helpful to you."

"I am not a project that you have to complete," Scott said. "I will be fine, really."

"Is that what you think?" Bill asked. "That you are just some task I am looking to check off my list?"

"Isn't that why you are doing all this?" Scott asked. "You are trying to convince me of something, make me see something that I have been missing the whole time. I appreciate what you are trying to do, but you don't have to save us, Bill."

Bill paused and sighed. He continued to gaze out into the darkness. They stood for a long time in silence, looking out over the land.

"I love coming out here," Bill said at last. "It reminds me of my purpose."

"Your purpose?" Scott asked.

"You think you understand what I am trying to do," Bill said. "But you really have no idea. None at all."

"What do you mean?"

Bill paused for a moment. Finally, he spoke again.

"Scott, can I tell you one more story? I think it might help you."

Scott sighed and rubbed his eyes.

"I suppose I can stand one more."

"I'm glad," Bill said. "Because this one is my own."

A Note from the Author

You can discover the power of a charitable remainder trust—an increasingly popular structure utilized by philanthropists worldwide.

Join individuals like Stuart and Joyce, who have found a way to make a lasting impact on drinking water accessibility in Africa through this innovative model. By establishing a charitable remainder trust, they were not only able to make an initial contribution that resulted in substantial tax benefits but also secured an ongoing annual income for themselves throughout the life of the trust.

This unique setup allowed Stuart and Joyce to continue supporting their chosen cause while enjoying financial stability. When the trust concludes, the remaining assets are generously bestowed upon the very charity that has been close to their hearts.

You can also unlock the potential of a charitable partnership structure and unleash the force of your contributions to make a lasting impact on worthy organizations worldwide. By embracing the power of a charitable partnership, you can join forces with experts and like-minded individuals, pooling resources and expertise to shape the future of the charitable organizations closest to your heart.

For a streamlined and effective approach, few options rival the donor-advised fund. Follow in the footsteps of Nicole and Randall, who harnessed this powerful mechanism to champion critical Alzheimer's research. With a donor-advised fund, you retain ultimate control over where and how your contributions are allocated, while entrusted professionals manage the intricate logistics and administration. This empowers you to make informed decisions while ensuring your philanthropic journey remains smooth and impactful.

By embracing the potential of a charitable remainder trust or charitable partnership or exploring the possibilities of a donor-advised fund, you can maximize the reach and effectiveness of your giving. Consult with a trusted financial advisor to navigate these avenues and discover how you can optimize your philanthropic efforts, leaving a meaningful and lasting legacy with the causes that matter most to you.

Discussion Questions

1. After taking care of your own family, how do you want to use your wealth to benefit others?

2. What three things do you need to accomplish that goal?

a.

b.

c.

Is a charitable lead trust or a charitable remainder trust better suited for your goals? Find out more by visiting www.IncreaseYourWorth.org.

Want to learn more about Legacy Income Trusts? See our 'Resources' chapter at the end of this book.

CHAPTER 5

"You know, Scott, our lives are not that different," Bill said.

"They look a lot different from where I am standing," Scott replied.

Bill nodded in response.

"Appearances can be deceiving. On first glance you might make a judgment about someone, maybe that is what you did with me."

"Are you saying you never make snap judgments based on first impressions? That you never did that with me?"

"I suppose I did," Bill said. "I suppose we all do that in some way or another."

He paused.

"But now I see that we have a lot more in common than I would have expected. You are facing a significant life decision, Scott, and you are the only one who is qualified to make it. No matter how much advice you hear from me or anyone else, just remember that this decision ultimately belongs to you."

"I realize that," Scott said. "And that is the problem."

"You want to eschew responsibility?" Bill asked.

"I want the decision to become apparent to me," Scott said. "All these stories you tell, listening to Joyce and Stuart earlier – I keep hearing over and over again that the decision was obvious, like it was destiny all along, like there could have been only one outcome and all they had to do was walk into it."

"But it was never like that," Bill said. "It never is. Decisions seem obvious only in retrospect. Only in the retelling of their story do Joyce and Stuart see how obvious the decision was. It is clear to them *now*, and only after everything that followed. I can guarantee you that they struggled with this as much as you did."

"How do you know that?"

"Because I was faced with a similar decision, years ago, and I struggled."

"You mean, you don't have all the answers waiting at your fingertips?" Scott joked.

Bill chuckled softly.

"I am not a particularly smart man," he said. "But I learned years ago that if I could just surround myself with people smarter than I am – my friends, colleagues, the books I read – that maybe I didn't need to be the smartest person alive. I just needed the humility to accept help and guidance from others."

"And you're saying I have too much pride to accept help," Scott said.

"Not at all," Bill replied. "I don't know how much of this will be useful to you. I am talking about myself now. When I was younger, I was too prideful to accept the wisdom of others. I thought I could do it all on my own."

"And how did that work out for you?"

"Not well," Bill said. "Not well at all."

Bill paused for a moment, allowing the words to settle between them. After a brief silence, he continued.

"For many years I worked as a real estate developer. Mostly commercial spaces, retail, shopping centers, things you have seen in every city in the United States. And I was very good at my job. But after a while, the stress of my work began to take its toll. Negotiating multi-million-dollar land deals will do that to you."

"It sounds stressful," Scott said.

"Fortunately, I had a property on the coast where Martha and I would go when we needed to escape the challenges of work. We would take off for a weekend, or occasionally even a full week, and it would feel like paradise out there. It was a small home, nothing too elaborate, and I had purchased it early in my career when I landed my first big deal. A gift, to myself and to Martha."

"That sounds very nice," Scott said.

"It was."

"But what does that have to do with what I am going through?" Scott asked.

"I was young and ambitious at the time," Bill said. "Always looking for that next deal, working all the time. After a while, I stopped going out there, and when we stopped going out there, we decided to use the property to generate some rental income, which is what we did. It was a nice little business for us, another investment that grew our wealth."

"Do you still have the house?"

"No," Bill said. "Over time, the value of the home skyrocketed. That is the thing about buying a house on the coast. We were one of the first owners in that area, and after a while development started and it became a destination. The value of the home more than tripled, so we decided it made more sense to sell than to keep it as a rental."

"That's great," Scott said. "So, you found yourself with a windfall – what charity did you support?"

"Scott, I was a long way from where I am today," Bill said. "I still had a lot to learn."

"What do you mean?"

"I was a lot like you, not wanting to make a mistake, trying to hold onto what I had. Of course, at the time I didn't have the friends I have now, I was too busy to pick up a book and read for anything other than advancing my career."

"So, what did you do? What did you decide?"

"Nothing," Bill said. "I didn't know what to do, so I did nothing."

"Nothing?"

"Exactly. And that was the worst decision I could have made. We saw a lot of our wealth get wiped out by taxes – a significant amount, Scott. Had I known then what I know now, we could have made a much better plan. But you can only proceed with the information you have at the time. As you know very well."

Bill paused for a moment. He stared into the distance as though reliving the pain of that decision. Then he sighed and shook his head.

"For the longest time, I tried to do it all by myself, and I lost a lot along the way. Not just financially, although that was a big part. But my relationships suffered as well. I didn't think I could turn to anyone for help. It seemed like it was my problem to solve, and I felt terrible because I couldn't produce the right answer. And I was a person who always took pride in having the right answer. I had spent years making the right plays, and now here I was with no idea what to do next."

"So, what is this, a cautionary tale?"

Bill smiled.

"I was young back then. But if there is one thing, I can say for myself, it is that I learn lessons well. Everything that happened to us back then has informed the decisions Martha and I make today."

"What decisions?"

"Just a moment," Bill said, holding up his hand in a friendly gesture. "I am getting to that part. Things were changing all around me back then, I was making development deals left and right, business was booming, I could not have been more successful if I tried. Or so I thought."

"What does that mean?"

"I started looking at the world differently, started reading books again that were outside of my scope. I started reading Thoreau and John Muir, Wendell Berry, and I discovered a real passion for wild spaces, for the efforts to preserve wilderness for other species, for future generations, for the good of the earth. Wendell Berry wrote about the difference between a road and a path, and suddenly I was seeing things as though for the first time. Have you read much of his work?"

"No," Scott admitted.

"Borrow another book before you leave here tonight," Bill said. "If nothing else, it is great writing."

He paused again and then continued.

"So, there I was, one of the best developers in the country, tearing down natural land to build more and more, and I started asking the questions of purpose and meaning – I mean, how many malls can one man create? Those types of things. I started having trouble sleeping at night."

"Waking up in a panic, like you forgot something?" Scott asked.

"Heart crashing in my chest," Bill said. "For a while I thought I was having a heart attack until finally one night I took myself to the emergency room, convinced that if I didn't go, I was going to die. I remember telling Martha as I sat on the edge of the bed that I thought I was having a heart attack, and as I said those words, I remember thinking that there were so many more things that I wanted to accomplish, things that were outside of my successful career. Dreams that Martha and I had shared for years but had not yet begun."

"Was it a heart attack?"

Bill smiled.

"It was a panic attack," he said. "They told me that I was carrying around a lot of stress, but that my heart was in perfect health. I needed to sleep more, relax more, maybe take some time away from work, meditate – all the things they recommend when your body is going into a full-shock panic. They told me that if I didn't slow down and change my habits, that it could develop into something more serious."

He turned and looked at Scott with an intensity that Scott had not seen before. Normally he was affable, smiling, always on the verge of telling a joke. But now his green eyes burned bright.

"You cannot continue this way, Scott. You need to sleep and you need to find ways to calm yourself. You are too young and have too much left to do to go dying on us all."

Scott laughed uncomfortably, but Bill did not smile. He stared at him intently.

"I will do my best," Scott said.

Bill nodded.

"Good," he said. Then he returned to his story.

"In a perfect world, that would have been the end of it. I would have retired from development, settled down with Martha and our son, Richard, I would have spent my time coaching his little league team and doing projects around the house."

"But that doesn't sound like something you would have wanted," Scott said.

"I couldn't slow down," Bill said. "Not all at once, anyway. But what that moment did was shake me loose, force me to look at not just *what* I was doing, but *why*. And it occurred to me that one of my core responsibilities was to help others in need. To do my part to help the world."

"Further the common good," Scott said.

"The only question was – what do I want to do?" Bill said.

"I ask that question all the time," Scott said.

"Well, during all this, we moved out here to this home," Bill said, sweeping his arm to cover the property. "It was a dream home for us, the perfect place for Richard to grow, and we loved it."

He gazed out onto the wildlands below.

"And out there, I saw nothing but opportunity."

"Opportunity?" Scott asked.

"I hate to admit this," Bill said. "But I was still a successful developer. I saw land and thought of all the possibilities that it could hold. I thought of what could go down there."

He paused for a moment, reliving his vision in his mind.

"Creekside Commons," he said. "A multi-use housing and retail space. It would have been perfect."

"Let me get this straight," Scott said. "You were going to turn all that land into a shopping center?"

"I bought the land and was ready to go," Bill said. "But then I kept finding myself awake at night. The panic attacks had slowed, but I was still not sleeping enough. I would rise in the middle of the night and go check on Richard, then pick up a book and carry it out to the deck and sit here and read. And listen to the sounds below."

Bill closed his eyes and breathed deeply. Then he opened his eyes and smiled.

"Sometimes, if you are really lucky, you are given a second chance to make the right decision."

"What decision was that?" Scott said.

"I suddenly owned all this land," Bill said. "And the longer I held it, the greater its value. It was the beach house all over again. Except this time, I was determined to have a different outcome. I just needed to know how to do that."

"What did you do?"

"I talked to my friends. I read books. Because of my previous experiences, I was able to find the humility to ask for help, and my friends had the grace to help me. They wanted to see me make the right decision, too. I was getting older, Scott. Maybe a bit wiser, too. I started making friends with people who were as successful as I was – in many ways, they were *more* successful than I was.

They directed me to Stickney Research."

"Stickney Research?" Scott said.

"They simplified the entire wealth management process," Bill said. "In fact, it was their educational resources that finally unlocked everything for me."

"How did they do that?"

"It wasn't like other financial advisors, who simply showed me what decisions they thought I should make. They taught me the process of decision-making itself. The team at Stickney Research were the first ones who broke down the issue in a way that gave me clarity – they helped me understand my goals, and then they showed me exactly how I could achieve them."

Bill paused for a moment before continuing.

"We are all searching for significance, Scott. That is what keeps you up at night. It's not the money, or the taxes, or whether this or that charity is the right call, or which type of trust you should use. Those are all worthy questions to ask – but it is not *the question*. The single question that drives you, that will continue to drive you whether you work another 30 years or never work another day in your life. It is the question of significance. That is the common thread that runs through a lot of the stories I am sharing with you."

"All those friends of yours?" Scott said.

"They became my friends, yes," Bill said. "And we all had one thing in common. Warren helped each of us realize how we could have a greater impact on our own lives and the lives of the people around us. A greater impact on the world. That is how I learned about the summer resort, the church giving, the animal sanctuary, and half a dozen other stories I *didn't* share with you."

"We would be out here all night," Scott said.

Bill laughed.

"When I learn something valuable, I can't help it. I feel compelled to share it with people I care about."

He paused.

"I spent months working with Stickney Research, going through all the scenarios, really digging into the decisions and what would be the best structure to achieve my biggest goals. And that is when I thought about this place."

"This place here?" Scott asked.

"I was finally in a place where I could make the right decision."

"And what did you decide?"

Bill smiled again. His eyes gleamed the way they always did when he wanted to share good news.

"I gave it away, Scott."

"You did what?"

"I created a charitable remainder trust and donated the land to a non-profit committed to preserving wild spaces. The land is untouchable now, Scott."

"What?" Scott said. "All this out here? You own this land?"

Bill shook his head.

"No," he said. "That is not the point. The point is that nobody owns the land. We are stewards of the land, preserving it for future generations. Years after I first created the charitable remainder trust, I wanted to do more to ensure it would remain safe even after I was gone. I had just negotiated the final deal of my career, the South Creek Mall."

"We have shopped there many times – that was yours?"

"One more shopping mall," Bill said. "But that allowed me to reinvest, to start a family foundation. We are now the stewards of this land. It is written in our mission statement. I sit on the board and will continue to do so until I am gone. And still, the land will live on. Years and years from now when you and I are long gone, people can still walk to their back decks and breathe this sweet night air. People can still explore the wilderness below, and marvel at the beauty of an unspoiled creek and the animals that call it home."

"You weren't worried to give it all away like that?"

"At first, yes," Bill said. "Until I learned how a charitable remainder trust worked. I was a lot like you when it came time to plan my wealth. I wanted to leave a legacy but feared I would need that money over time. I wanted to do something important and meaningful but was just torn up about what to do. What would happen if I became sick, or Martha was sick, or we needed that money down the road?"

"But you did it anyway?" Scott asked.

"It was the perfect solution," Bill said. "The elegant solution. By using a charitable remainder trust, we have created a long, long-range plan. We accumulate money in the trust and still have access to income from it should we need it. But in the end, it goes to our family foundation where future generations can steward what we started and protect the land."

Bill gazed over the wilderness. He began to speak from memory:

> *I met a traveller from an antique land,*
> *Who said—'"Two vast and trunkless legs of stone*
> *Stand in the desert. . . . Near them, on the sand,*
> *Half sunk a shattered visage lies, whose frown,*
> *And wrinkled lip, and sneer of cold command,*
> *Tell that its sculptor well those passions read*
> *Which yet survive, stamped on these lifeless things,*
> *The hand that mocked them, and the heart that fed;*
> *And on the pedestal, these words appear:*
> *My name is Ozymandias, King of Kings;*
> *Look on my Works, ye Mighty, and despair!*
> *Nothing beside remains. Round the decay*
> *Of that colossal Wreck, boundless and bare*
> *The lone and level sands stretch far away."*

"Look," he said. "I cannot tell you what to do with this decision, Scott. Your fate is entirely within your hands. All I can tell you is that I have been there before – twice – and I have seen the results from both sides. We cannot spend our lives building monuments to ourselves. They become insignificant over time. The only way to make a lasting impact is to help others. To help the next generation. If you can do that, you'll have no regrets. Trust me."

"Thank you, Bill."

"I hope this has been helpful to you. I know what a significant decision you are facing, but I trust that you will make the right choice."

"Do well by doing good, right?" Scott said.

Bill smiled.

"Exactly," he said.

The conversations were beginning to die down behind them, and Joyce and Stuart were preparing to go home. Carol looked across the deck at Scott and he held up his hand to signal he would be there soon.

"Thank you for your help, Bill," he said. "I really appreciate it."

"You know," Bill said. "There was a time when I thought maybe you didn't like me very much."

Scott chuckled.

"I think that had more to do with me than anything else," he said.

Bill nodded and wished Scott a good evening. They shook hands and then Scott turned to leave.

"Oh, Scott?" Bill said.

Scott turned around.

"Yes?"

"There was one more thing I forgot to mention, about my decision."

"What is that?"

"On the day I finally made it, I slept," he said. "Best night of sleep I ever had."

"Good night," Scott said.

"Be well," Bill replied.

Scott and Carol exited Jones Manor and walked slowly toward their home. They entered the dark entryway and discovered a light still on in the kitchen. The girls were still awake and sitting around the kitchen table, eating snacks and talking.

"How was the party?" Savannah asked.

"It was good," Carol said. Turning to Scott, she asked, "Was it good?"

"It was," Scott said.

He and Carol joined the girls at the table and Scott picked up a handful of crackers and chewed thoughtfully on them while his daughters chatted. Finally, he spoke again.

"I think I know what to do now," Scott said. "Something that can help us and help a lot of people at the same time."

He looked at Savannah.

"An opportunity for people to make something for themselves. To help children, just like you."

"You really know?" His daughters asked.

"It has been a long journey," Scott said. "And an even longer one ahead. But yes, I do."

A Note from the Author

It is possible to unlock the true potential of your wealth and maintain control over your financial legacy through the creation of a charitable trust.

By establishing a trust, such as a charitable remainder trust (CRT), you gain the power to determine precisely where your hard-earned money is allocated, ensuring your values and goals are upheld.

Just like Bill, who initially utilized a CRT but expanded his philanthropic efforts by establishing a private foundation, you can make an even greater impact by setting up a platform that is bound to fulfill the specific mission you envision. By actively serving on the foundation's Board of Directors, as Bill does, you retain a direct influence on shaping your ongoing legacy, ensuring that your charitable endeavors align with your evolving vision.

Navigating the intricacies of charitable trusts and wealth management can be complex, so it is highly recommended to discuss this option with a trusted financial advisor. They can provide personalized guidance and expertise to help you make informed decisions and maximize the benefits of your charitable giving – giving you the opportunity to utilize your wealth to create a profound impact on your community or the world at large and empower others to succeed alongside you.

Remember, inaction guarantees the loss of your decision-making power, resulting in the government assuming control over your assets and leaving you without a voice in how they are utilized. You can seize the chance to make a difference and secure your lasting influence by taking proactive steps towards creating a charitable trust.

Discussion Questions

1. What does 'enable to the difference' mean to you?

2. How much control do you want to have over how your wealth is used in the future?

CHAPTER 6

After several years, the big day had finally arrived.

Scott stood in front of the mirror, getting ready, checking his appearance. He was older now, a bit of gray starting to appear in his brown hair, and silver strands in the beard he had grown a year earlier. Carol said it made him look distinguished.

Now he tightened his red and blue checkered tie against his white shirt. Carol entered the room and walked up behind him, and for a moment they stood smiling at each other in the mirror.

"Almost time to go," she said.

Scott nodded and smiled. Although years had passed, his face looked younger somehow, lighter. He felt less troubled, more joyful and at peace.

He stepped out onto the third-story patio of the hotel. Outside there was a cool spring breeze and below the hotel he could see the dense green foliage and red-roofed houses of the villages below. In the distance he could just make out the blue waters of Lake Victoria.

It was their second trip to Uganda. The first had taken place when they were breaking ground at the school, and now here they were again, all this time later, ready to open for the first time. He breathed deeply and stretched his arms over his head. It had indeed been a long journey. Flying out of Seattle, nearly 14 hours overnight before landing at Hamad International in Qatar, curling up on lounge seating before being called to their next flight, a relatively short 5-hour trip to Entebbe.

But they were there, and as he closed his eyes and breathed the fresh air and felt the cool breeze and listened to the trees and the water and the sounds of traffic moving below, he knew that he had done the right thing. He never in his life could have imagined that all of this would have led him to a seaside city in Uganda, preparing to take a car ride through the country's interior to a small village, where he had helped create something where there was once nothing. That his legacy would be felt across the world from where he started.

He thought back to decades earlier, beginning his humble career at New Wave Technologies. How could he have known back then all the possibilities that life held? And yet here he was, standing in a country that had for most of his life been a place on a map, living and breathing in a world that suddenly seemed so much bigger than he could have ever imagined. He smiled and opened his eyes and looked around him again.

What could he feel except an enormous, almost incomprehensible sense of gratitude?

Savannah walked outside and joined Scott on the deck. They stood together in silence, watching the trees in the distance.

"Mom said we need to get going," Savannah said. "Emily just finished getting ready, and Mom said we should go now if we want to make it in time for the ceremony."

"Thank you," Scott said. He placed an arm around Savannah, who was taller now, older. But still his little girl.

"Isn't this beautiful out here?" He said. "Can you believe we are standing here right now? How could one day be so beautiful?"

"Come on, Dad," Savannah said. "Save your mushy speeches for someone else."

But even as she said it, there was a smile in her voice.

They left the room and took the elevator down to the lobby, where a group of workers were setting out snacks and drinks for the guests. Scott considered stopping for a quick bite to eat, but Savannah was right, they needed to keep moving. They walked out the front doors and to the parking lot, where Carol was already seated in the driver's seat. They climbed into the car and she pulled away from the hotel and started down the street, leaving their multi-story building in the rear view. Soon they were outside of the city of Entebbe and making their way northwest along the Kampala-Hoima Road. It would be three hours of driving before they reached their destination.

As they drove past towns and villages, Scott looked out the window at the passing homes and buildings, the green spaces, and the farmlands. A lot had changed in the past few years, yet the things that mattered had remained intact. He was sleeping better all the time. Bill was right, as soon as he made his decision, he slept in a way that he never had before. And each morning feeling free, and purely happy.

He thought of the events that had led him to his decision, the stories that Bill had told him, the dinners at Jones Manor, the moment that he finally arrived at the understanding that he knew without a doubt what he needed to do. He tried to remember the person he was before the decision, the person who was sleepless and worried, anxious over everything, angry at himself and the world. That all seemed so far away, now. He smiled.

He thought of his own family, the girls growing up, Emily going off to college, the quiet days with Carol in the house, taking weekend trips together, spending time in the evening with Savannah, either talking about what she was learning in school or her friends or the volunteering she had started doing every other weekend with a conservation group. She wanted to study environmental science when she entered college. Scott thought with pride about how he would be able to afford to send the girls to college, and that he and Carol would be comfortable and well supported the rest of their lives. He thought about the legacy they would leave when they were gone.

Without realizing it, he had daydreamed away the long drive. Hours had passed without his noticing them, and now they had arrived at the site of a brand-new school. As they pulled into the long pathway leading to the buildings, they could see out the window the large monument sign:

Scott Davis Academy

The grounds were immaculately maintained, with red clay paths dotted with mature growth shade trees – the perfect place to lie outside with a book and study or talk with friends during the lunch period and after school. They parked on an open square of dirt, the red dust rising around their car, and Scott stepped outside to see the beautiful main building. Its fresh tan walls and red roofing stood in stark contrast to the brilliant blue sky. A crowd had already gathered. Classrooms flanked the main building on either side, and in front was a gathering area.

They parked the car and walked toward the entrance of the main building, greeting well-wishers as they went. Most were families, with some members of the community, even some of the city leaders made an appearance. The children were wearing new school uniforms and beaming with pride.

Scott, Carol, Savannah, and Emily were led through the crowd to the entrance of the main hall. The head of the school met them at the entrance.

"Big moment," he said, smiling.

"Did you know this many people were going to show up?" Emily asked.

"I had no idea," Scott said. He embraced his eldest daughter." I am so glad we are here."

The school principal shook Scott's hand and then walked them through the main entrance. There was still time before the official ceremony, and he wanted to show them the grounds. Off the main entrance were hallways leading in both directions, and down the halls were a series of identical classrooms.

The classrooms were furnished with carefully swept stone floors and wood benches for the children, and at the front of the classroom were two large blackboards, where the teachers had already written instructions for the first day of school.

Scott and his family walked silently through the school rooms while the principal explained what they would be learning. He explained that until the school had opened, thousands of school children could not earn an education in Uganda. They did not have the facilities to teach them.

"You have given them a great opportunity," he said. "We cannot thank you enough."

Scott smiled and looked at Savannah and Emily. He put his arms around his girls.

"They were the inspiration, right here," he said.

They continued touring the facilities and eventually the principal walked them outside. There, water downspouts were attached to the buildings and ran directly into large black containers, preserving water for use throughout the school.

Farther away from the school there were several acres of farmland, precisely plowed and furrowed in straight rows.

"Not only have you given the children a chance to learn," the principal said. "But you have provided them with the means to make something for their village. This is a working farm, and the food that is produced here will go back to the families who need it most. Soon, we will have water wells drilled onto the property, which will continue the development of this special place."

They concluded their campus tour and returned to the main entrance, where now a large group was waiting for them. Rows of spectators stretched back in the distance away from the entrance, everyone gathering to catch a glimpse of the ceremony.

Scott and his family stood to one side while the school principal walked up three steps to the stone entrance, where they had erected a small stage. He arranged his notes behind a podium. He introduced himself and then made a few remarks:

> "What do you need to be a successful school? To be a successful student? Is it an abundance of material goods?

I don't believe that it is.

A great school is one in which teachers genuinely care about their students. A great school is one in which friendships and relationships are formed that can last a lifetime. Students, when you go to Scott Davis Academy you can know, without any doubt, that the teachers and staff on this campus are working all the time for your benefit, that they want to help you succeed. When you are a Scott Davis Academy student, you are part of a greater community. When you are a Scott Davis Academy student, you are known. That is one area where our teachers do so well; they spend time understanding their students. We want the education that our students receive to be exceptional – for them.

And parents, a great school is one that is built on respect. That is a cornerstone at Scott Davis Academy. But listen, when I say the word respect, I do not mean a set of rules governing behavior. I do not mean blind obedience. I mean that we care about your children; they are not our own but we will treat them as though they were. When you watch the children walk to their classrooms and shake their teacher's hand, know that they are not just following some antiquated rule. They are building a relationship. When you walk into a classroom and the entire class rises to greet you, know that they are not being forced into politeness. They are honoring you.

Students, I will give you one secret about how to live a successful life – and particularly at this school. When you follow the rules that we have set forth at Scott Davis Academy – when you live your life with respect and honor – you will find that you are not limited in any way. Rather, you become free. You become free to learn, to explore, to build meaningful and lasting relationships with your classmates and friends. Rules are not meant to restrict you but to allow you the freedom to become your best self.

But that is not everything that goes into a great school. It is simply the beginning. Without respect – among staff, among students, among parents – it all begins slowly to erode away.

A great school is also built in the pursuit of personal excellence. This can often be a challenging journey, filled with many distractions, setbacks, and disappointments. The writer Donald Miller in his book A Million Miles in a Thousand Years, describes a person's life story like paddling a boat away from shore:

"The first part happens fast ... and you're finally out on the water, the shore is receding behind you and the trees are getting smaller. The distant shore doesn't seem too far, and you can feel the resolution coming, the feeling of getting out of the boat and walking the distant beach. You think that it will happen fast, that you will paddle for a bit and get to the other side by lunch. But the truth is, it isn't going to be over soon. The reward you get is always less than you thought it would be, and the work is always harder than you imagined. The point of the story is never the ending, though. It is about your character getting molded in the hard work of the middle."

We all want to change the world. We all want to be successful. We just want to do it from the shore. It's human nature. It takes some courage just to step into the boat and begin those first tentative strokes away from the land. But the real work is done in the middle, when it is dark, so dark that you cannot see either shore, and you have to trust only in your own abilities and that you are moving in the right direction.

Students, you may find yourself out in that water this year. You may get started on a journey toward personal excellence and find that the water is rough and you cannot see, and you are ready to give up. But at Scott Davis Academy, you are not alone in your journey. There is always a teacher to shine a light for you, to tell you that it is not as far as you think. There is always a friend to pick up another oar.

But listen, everyone, we cannot give up! That is the lesson! If we focus our attention entirely on external goals – on the shore instead of our work – then we will not succeed. It is good to set goals. I encourage all of you to set goals this year. They keep us focused and honest with ourselves. But don't let the goal be the only focus. Let personal excellence be your focus this year.

Thomas Edison, depending on which historical account you read, failed anywhere from 700 to 10,000 when trying to design a viable lightbulb. At one point a reporter allegedly asked him how it felt to fail 1000 times to invent the light bulb. He replied, I did not fail 1000 times. The light bulb is an invention with 1000 steps.

When you set a goal this year, don't give up! If you experience setbacks, remind yourself to keep rowing! You will reach it. You have the support of your family and friends. You have the support of your teachers. You have my support.

That is what a great school offers. We do not have an abundance of material goods, but we have each other. We have the relationships that we will build this year. We have the support that we will give each other, and especially to our students, as they venture forth on the next part of their great life adventure.

In this sense, we are a bit like George Bailey in It's a Wonderful Life. We are the richest school in town.

And of course, on this first day of school, we would be remiss if we did not recognize the family who made this all possible. Scott Davis and his family represent the values that our school will foster in its students every day. Scott Davis had a vision for a better future, and he did everything within his power to bring that vision to life.

Because of the Davis family, we stand here on the steps of our beautiful grounds, preparing to embark on a great journey together. We have a school site that will serve students from this village for generations to come – tuition-free. And because of Mr. Davis's particular foresight, students at this school will take specific classes in community building, financial literacy, and stewardship, ensuring that the children who graduate the Scott Davis Academy move forward into young adulthood equipped with the tools and knowledge to pursue their greatest dreams.

Students, parents, and staff, may the respect that we foster this year grow into unbreakable integrity, may our pursuit of knowledge and excellence grow into wisdom, and may our characters be forever strengthened by the work that we do this year.

Scott Davis Academy is a great school. May our students learn to live lives of great meaning and virtue, and to become difference makers in the world around them."

The crowd erupted into applause at the conclusion of the principal's speech, and then he stepped to one side and gestured for Scott and his family to come to the center. A large red ribbon stretched across the entrance to the main building. Several people moved the podium away from the stage to give the crowd an unobstructed view of the ribbon cutting.

"Mr. Davis," the principal said, smiling. "Thank you, for everything."

He handed Scott an oversized set of scissors, and Scott, Carol, and the girls all placed their hands together on the handles.

"This is incredible," Savannah said. "I never thought I would be doing something like this."

"Yes," Scott said. "This feels like a dream, doesn't it?"

Together they clipped the scissors across the ribbon, letting it fall gently to the ground while the crowd cheered their approval.

There were more words spoken by prominent members of the Ndagga village, as well as a few student speakers. Then Scott and his family moved into the crowd and the inaugural class of the Scott Davis Academy took their places on the steps of the main hall to perform a school song. They had learned it months earlier in preparation for the big day, and they beamed with nervous pride while they stood on the steps and their parents snapped pictures and shot video.

INCREASE YOUR WORTH

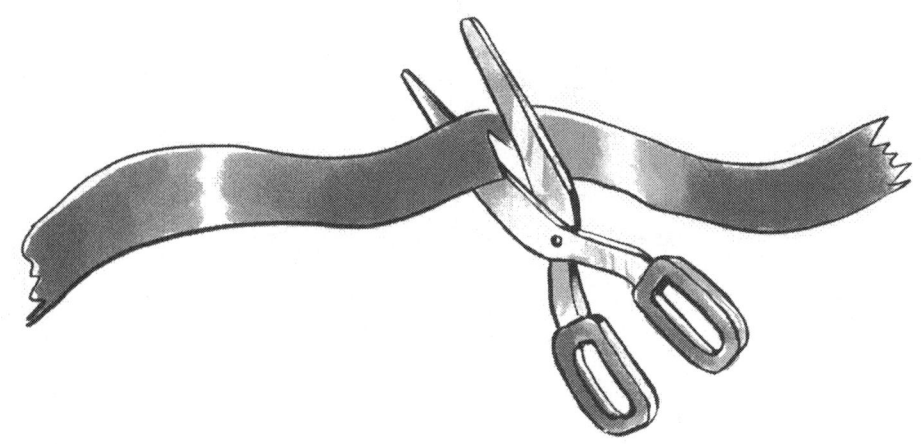

At the teacher's command, they broke into a spirited rendition of the school song. There was great fanfare as the student choir sang beautifully in celebration of the day. All around him, Scott felt the joy from the families. Savannah was right. It was incredible. Scott smiled to himself and closed his eyes, listening to the wonderful sounds.

Then, suddenly, he felt a presence beside him. He opened his eyes and turned to see a man smiling directly into his eyes. He was older, but there was no mistaking the bright green eyes.

"Bill Jones," Scott said. "What are you doing here?"

Bill smiled. "I wouldn't dare miss this. I knew you would make the right decision."

Scott laughed. "With just a little help."

Bill suddenly dropped his smile and looked serious.

"Scott," he said. "There is something I have been meaning to ask you."

"What's that, Bill?"

"Does this mean we're friends now?" He asked. Then he broke into a big grin. "Because if not, you owe me a Benjamin Franklin biography."

Scott put his hand on Bill's shoulder.

"Not a chance, Bill."

They smiled and stood together with Scott's family while the children sang. It was the most beautiful spring day of the year.

A Note from the Author

Discover the transformative power of philanthropy and find your own meaningful purpose, inspired by the remarkable journey of Scott Davis, guided by the expertise of Bill Jones and the unwavering support of his family.

By establishing a charitable trust, Scott secured the essential funding necessary to bring his vision to life - the Scott Davis Academy. This groundbreaking institution not only provides education but does so in a tuition-free manner, ensuring accessibility for generations to come.

The ingenious structure of the trust also allows Scott to receive a modest annual income, enabling him to sustain his personal livelihood while dedicating himself wholeheartedly to his noble cause. By retaining his decision-making power, Scott has become an agent of profound change in a village desperately in need.

Join Scott and countless others in creating a lasting impact by exploring the possibilities of a charitable trust. To navigate this empowering journey with confidence and expertise, it is highly recommended to consult a trusted financial advisor who can guide you through the intricacies of setting up a charitable trust and help you make informed decisions aligned with your values and aspirations.

Together, let us embrace the opportunity to make a significant difference in the lives of those who need it most, while securing our own lasting legacies.

The Big Question

1. What kind of difference do you want to have in the world?

Find out how you can achieve your philanthropic goals and take control of your wealth by visiting www.IncreaseYourWorth.org.

CONCLUSION

While all of the characters in the book faced different challenges, they all shared something in common; the willingness to learn and to embrace new ideas and new possibilities. Whenever we learn and grow, opportunities may appear that once seemed only available to the super rich or available to us only with a great compromise. My hope is that in reading the various vignettes you can see that in every case their financial and life situations, as well as personal worth and value, are increased by employing the tools of a charitable remainder trust, a charitable lead trust and a Pooled Income Fund. These are powerful tools which allow one to give money away and retain what is oftentimes the most important benefit - control of income from the very asset given away!

When we think about life's challenges in terms of retirement and financial independence, it's not the principal that matters; it's the cash flow. And the cash flow is what enables our dreams. The use of a split interest trust (i.e., charitable remainder, charitable lead or pooled income fund) when used in conjunction with thoughtful planning will significantly leverage and increase wealth. A person once asked me, "if there was a pile of a million dollars sitting on the table and it cost me $50,000 to take control of that pile, would I do it?" Of course, it didn't take me but a millisecond to say "yes, I want control of that million dollars!" That is exactly the type of dilemma, which to me is not a dilemma, that we all face. When we look at our W-2 or tax return, we notice a significant amount is being either given away or taken away, depending on your viewpoint, whereby you lose complete control and have no vote as to what happens with the money. In contrast, by using the strategies outlined in this book we can recover and regain use of those funds and indeed make a real difference.

It is often said that a person's only regret on their deathbed is not what they've done in life, but what they haven't done. In talking to many people about their dreams and true purpose it always comes down to love; wanting to be loved and contribution to something bigger. Magically they go hand in hand. It's hard to be loved without giving love. And it's hard to make a contribution in the world without giving. Through the miracle of legislation passed in 1964 we can do both and make our lives and the people around us lives significantly better.

My hope is that you've enjoyed the book and it has sparked your own thoughts of purposeful wealth. Please look at the resource section where you will find more information and a sample document for educational purposes. We don't recommend you use it because it's a basic IRS document, but it shows you not only the validity of the concept, but the fact that the IRS felt so strongly about the concept as to provide a document which one could download on their website.

For more detailed information please visit our website, www.IncreaseYourWorth.org and become part of this growing, giving community.

RESOURCES

Introduction

Thank you for reading *Increase Your Worth*. If you are searching for more information on how you can make charitable giving a part of your financial future, you are in luck! In this chapter, you will find the resources you need to understand each of the three most common charitable giving entities, as well as details on how you can get started with your charitable giving strategy.

Although in the past these strategies have been available only to people with significant wealth, it is our mission to make this information available to everyone – regardless of income. In doing so, we hope to give you the tools to make more, give more, and live more.

Before starting your charitable giving journey, we recommend reviewing these resources with a professional financial planner. For more information on the resources that you find here, please visit IncreaseYourWorth.org.

Types of Contributions

What Can Be Contributed:

- Rental property
- Land
- Small, closely held businesses
- VC business interest
- Oil/Gas/Mineral rights
- Cryptocurrency
- Stocks & Grants*
- Bonds
- Options
- Cash*

The majority of Pooled Income Funds only allow for Cash or Securities to be contributed

What tax can be avoided:

When you sell any of the above assets that have a big gain then the tax can be significant, which is avoided by using a CRT. Note the following are the taxes being avoided are as of 2021:

- State Taxes (3-18%)
- Long-Term Capital Gains (15-23%)
- Ordinary Income (Short Term Capital Gains) (21-37%)
- Net Investment Income Tax (3.8%)

TYPES OF ENTITIES:

Overview:

Three of the most common entities – Charitable Remainder Trust, Charitable Lead Trust, and Pooled Income Fund – are detailed below. Review the differences among the three entities to determine which is most beneficial to your unique financial circumstances. <u>You can also deploy them all, they are not mutually exclusive.</u>

Details:

Charitable Remainder Trust (CRT) A charitable remainder trust has two beneficiaries. In most cases, one of them is you (and possibly your spouse), and the other is the qualified charity or tax-exempt organization you plan to support. During your lifetime you receive a set percentage of income from the charitable trust. Once you pass away, the charity then receives whatever is left over. (If your spouse was receiving income as well, he or she will continue receiving it until passing away.) One of the benefits of a charitable remainder trust is that you may be able to become the trustee and make decisions about the assets within the trust, including investment choices and other important matters. Unfortunately, charitable remainder trusts are irrevocable, but you may be able to change the beneficiaries depending on design. This allows you some degree of personal freedom, especially if you find a charity or non-profit that you feel is more deserving of your gift. With a charitable remainder trust you get to choose the amount of income you'll be paid from the trust on an annual basis. Depending upon the type of trust, you can value the assets for distribution purposes at the time the trust is funded or on an annual basis. Some beneficiaries choose to take more, but it's generally recommended to take no more than 10%. All realized profit from investment sales within the trust is not subject to capital gains or income tax. This is because you are benefiting a charity. Charitable trusts are especially helpful when it comes to highly appreciated assets with limited income-producing potential. By avoiding the capital gains tax, more money goes to your charity instead of Uncle Sam. You also get an income tax deduction because your CRT supports a charity. Please note, however, that income from trust assets paid to you is subject to federal income taxes, again depending on design.

Charitable Lead Trust (CLT) A charitable lead trust is basically the same concept as a charitable remainder trust, but in reverse. With a CLT, a charity receives a certain percentage of income every year. At the end of the trust term, whoever you've named as the beneficiary (a spouse or children) receives the assets that remain. A CLT offers the same advantages of a remainder trust, but the roles are reversed. Both charitable remainder trusts and charitable lead trusts offer a variety of advantages over traditional estate planning tools. Above all, they allow you to give back to society while still taking advantage of tax deductions and exclusion from capital gains taxes. There are numerous details and complex steps to take when looking at a charitable trust as an estate planning option. You should always find a trusted financial professional to help guide you through the process. They can usually refer you to a known estate planning attorney who will also help. Like all estate planning options, trusts have their pros and cons, but they're certainly a good option worth considering if you wish to save on taxes, support a good cause, and feel great about it in the process.

Pooled Income Funds (PIF) Pooled income funds are similar to CRTs in that they provide income to the donor and then the balance gets distributed to the charity after the donor's death. They are established to accept cash or securities from donors that will be managed in one pooled asset fund. The trusts give the donor an itemized federal income tax deduction based on the charitable remainder portion of the contributed property value. Each trust account then provides lifetime distributions to several beneficiaries, vs the CRT or CLT which can only have up to two beneficiaries.

Unlike a charitable annuity Trust where you receive a set income amount, the amount you receive under the PIF varies and depends on the performance of the investments held by the trust, regardless of the number of contributors to the fund. The fund takes into account IRS life expectancy tables and the fair market value of the assets at the time of the transfer to determine income tax deduction amounts. Unlike a NIMCRUT provision in the CRT, you must take a distribution every year. Upon the death of the last income beneficiary, the fund's remaining balance goes to his or her 501(c)(3) charity of choice.

One significant advantage to a PIF is that they generally have lower costs, more beneficiaries and less administrative complexity than charitable remainder trusts. This tool is often used to provide income stream to multiple generations and is useful in estate planning.

Benefits to Giving it Away

Overview:

The benefits are generally similar between a PIF, CRT and CLT. Keep in mind that each has a nuance and some advantages over the others, but keep in mind that there are almost an infinite number of variations depending on the type of asset contributed, how much of a gain there is, if the donor is single or married and what their age is, their income tax bracket and how much cash flow they desire. Nonetheless, following are the key benefits that a well-planned strategy and one of the tools above can provide:

- Asset protection since the trust is irrevocable and considered owned outside of your estate.
- Estate tax charitable deduction or possibly excluded from your estate entirely.
- Income stream to the donor (and in the case of the PIF, to multiple beneficiaries) for life
- No tax is due at sale of the asset, creating a larger pool of investable funds.
- Replacement of the asset with life insurance funded from the CRT income will benefit the family and provide a tax-free benefit, thus avoiding estate tax or sale of the asset.

Details:

How to Set up a CRT or CLT

Again, there are many variations to setting up the plan, but below are the basic steps to setting up a charitable trust:

1. Create the trust: Identify the donor (one person or married couple) and the asset. Identify the charity and define the terms of the trust (i.e., term and income).
2. Donate or transfer assets to the trust: this needs to take place before the property (in the case of real estate) is under sale contract. IRS rules will apply to timing of transfer and sale.
3. Trustee sells the asset and proceeds are tax free and go to the trust account controlled by the trustee.
4. The donor takes a tax deduction over a period of years and will be based on the asset value, age of donor and term of trust.

5. Trust pays income to the donor for life in the case of a CRT. With a Net-Income Make-up provision in the CRT (NIMCRUT), one can delay their income until they wish to turn it on – like an IOU from the trust to the donor. With a CLT, the charity is paid a specified donation annually for a specific term.
6. Donors may choose to fund life insurance to replace the asset that the family will not inherit using the income from the CRT.
7. Upon the donor's passing:
   a. With a CRT - the charity will receive the remainder of the assets held in the trust.
   b. With a CLT - the charity has received their donation over the term and anything left over goes back to the donor and his/her heirs.

How to set up a Pooled Income Fund Account

There are many sponsored plans available and since they already have the framework in place, it is very simple to set up your account.

1. Create an account with a PIF provider (sometimes the charity has one established) identifying the living beneficiaries for income and the charity beneficiary.
2. Donor contributes assets to the account.
3. Trust Fund distributes income to beneficiaries either concurrently, consecutively or a combination for their lifetime.
4. Upon the last income beneficiary's passing, the charity receives the remaining assets in the account.

Safe Harbor Rules

Because of the nature of the trust in providing income, the IRS has released specimen "safe harbor" forms for the charitable remainder trusts (CRUTs and CRATs). The sample forms are essentially safe harbors for drafting a CRT. This allows for taxpayers that a trust agreement which is "substantially similar" to one of the sample forms from its website will be recognized as meeting all of the requirements of a CRT. Therefore, it is not necessary to obtain a PLR (private letter ruling) to be assured that the charity's remainder interest is deductible.

All CRTs must name one or more qualified charitable organizations as remainder beneficiaries. And every CRT must provide for specific annual payments to one or more individuals for life or for a specific number of years. Once a trust is qualified, the tax law provides several tax benefits:

- The trust is exempt from paying taxes (unless there is income to it directly)
- The present value of the charitable remainder (the value less the projected income) is immediately deducted for income, estate and gift tax.
- Distributions to donors are taxed under a special provision of the law.

Obviously, the trust must qualify and that is the reason that the IRS has provided the sample documents outlining the provisions and code section to assist the taxpayer. These forms are basic and do not expand on trustee powers, gift-specific provisions, default positions, beneficiary changes, etc. That is left to the attorney to add. Given that there is now a requirement that every CRT have a remainder value equal to at least 10% of the initial value of the trust, that language should be added under a special provision when drafting a testamentary trust.

The trust document must provide income to the donor (first beneficiary) at least annually as stated above. The amount must be at least 5% of the value of the asset and as much as 50%. The date for valuation must be stated and the assets listed. As such, if the value of the underlying asset increases then the payment to the beneficiary should also increase. The present value of the remainder interest (that which is going to charity) qualifies as a charitable deduction for gift and estate tax, as well as income tax. Following is an example of a deduction for a one-life CRT. Note that these are based on 3% AFR and the rates change monthly. This is for illustration purposes only.

Percentage of Value Tax Deductible by Donor			
Age	Payout 5%	Payout 6%	Payout 7%
55	32%	26%	22%
60	38%	32%	28%
65	45%	39%	34%
70	52%	47%	42%
75	60%	55%	50%
80	68%	63%	59%

CASE STUDY #1

Jeff Tech is an employee of a large software company. He makes $365,000 a year in salary plus bonus and has vesting stock grants of $500,000 per year. The CRT strategy will provide a $500,000 investment bucket from which he can take $30,000 per year of distribution approximately. The use of the CRT can also give Mr. Tech tax savings of $193,000 to be directed to him instead of the IRS – and he'll have control over $500,000 to invest and enjoy. Here's a "before and after" chart illustrating the benefit.

Without a CRT		With a Leveraged CRT	
Salary & Bonus	$365,000	Salary	$365,000
Grants	$500,000	Grants	$500,000
Total Compensation	$865,000	Total Compensation	$865,000

		Leveraged CRT*	$500,000
Taxes	$337,000	Taxes	$144,000
FICA	$29,661	FICA	$29,661
Net Comp Received	$498,339	Net Comp Received	$191,339
		PLUS: CRT VALUE	$500,000
		Total in your control	$691,339

Mr. Tech will still control $691,339 of assets with $500,000 in the CRT to provide an income for life. He may also choose to defer this income until retirement. In exchange for his promise to give to charity whatever remains of the CRT assets after he takes withdrawals, Mr. Tech will receive sizeable tax savings. In having used the CRT, he has decreased his income tax liability upon exercise of vested grants, leaving him 58% more investable assets ($691,339) with which to generate a future income stream instead of the lesser amount ($438,339) that he would have had, with no plan.

CASE STUDY #2

John and Jane Sample are taking advantage of the hot real estate market. They want to sell their ski chalet. The real estate is worth $2 million and they bout it for $500,000. Therefore, if the Samples sell their investment real estate, they'll pay income tax on $1,500,000 of gain, assuming a combined federal and state capital gain rate of 33 percent, they will pay $500,000 in income taxes upon selling their investment real estate. If the Samples instead created a CRT and retitled the property in the CRT before the sale, they could sell their investment real estate free of current income tax, spread the cash flow and resulting tax liability over the remaining lifetimes and support their favorite charity or charities at the surviving spouse's death.

In addition, depending on their ages and certain structural decisions at the time of the transaction, they will also receive an income tax deduction of at least $700,000 in exchange for their promise to give whatever is left in the CRT to their favorite charities upon the surviving spouse's death. In other words, if the Samples promise to give the leftovers to charity upon the surviving spouse's death, the government will allow them to defer their income tax liability. In having used the CRT, they've sold their investment real estate free of current income tax, leaving them the full $2 million with which to generate a future income stream instead of just the $1.59 million they would have had after paying income taxes.

SAMPLE DIAGRAM OF CRT

Below is an example of moving stock into a CRT, but you can do so with real estate, cryptocurrency, artwork, etc. and the concept and example:

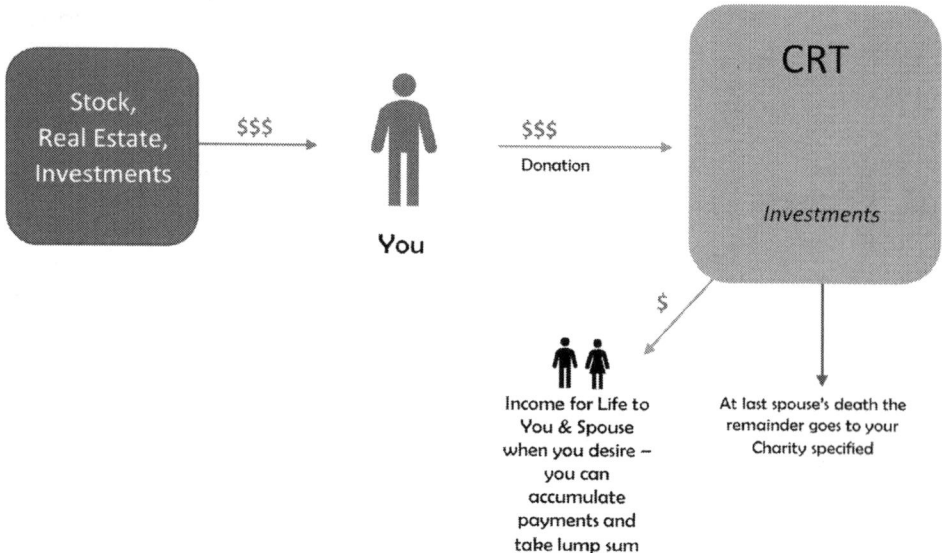

SAMPLE FAMILY FINANCIAL PHILOSOPHY

Oftentimes we will work with clients to create a family credo, outlining what they value and where they choose to leave a legacy.

A sample follows to help you start the conversation with your family.

Doe Family Financial Philosophy

SOURCES OF WEALTH

We feel that we were successful in building and growing a family business, which contributed to our family wealth. While hard work has paid off, we fully believe that assistance from family, support and teamwork from each other, and the financial success of our parents has played a significant role in our success.

RESPONSIBILITIES AND OBLIGATIONS

In examining the question of whether we feel financially secure, the answer is yes and no. John says "yes," because we certainly have resources and income to enjoy a secure life, but Jane feels that a true sense of financial independence is not quite achieved.

Given that our success is due to in part to our values, we both feel an obligation of our wealth to Family, Community and Charity.

When it comes to the distribution of our wealth, our first obligation is to each other, to secure our financial well-being and to avoid financial hardships. Additionally, we want to provide opportunities for our children and their future. We would like our children to have advantages, but also to lead productive lives.

Charities are to be included in the distribution of our wealth. Both of us feel our need to recognize this and provide for as we've been fortunate in our lives and would like to support those who are not.

PRIMARY PLANNING GOALS

Among our financial and estate planning goals that are most important to us, ensuring lifetime financial independence and maximizing inheritance for our heirs is our priority. After our immediate goals are met, we then wish to plan for estate tax minimization and charitable giving.

Among the five choices provided that might influence us to create or revise our current estate plan, having a better understanding about what we can accomplish with our financial resources is a priority for both of us followed by having a better understanding of our current financial status and the future needs of our family. Given our charitable inclination, we would like to have a better understanding of the tax benefits of giving to charitable or philanthropic organizations. We feel that an understanding of tax-effective estate planning options will facilitate many of our goals and that is an underlying desire that affects each of the areas previously stated.

Ideally, if we could minimize or eliminate taxes, we would like to distribute 80-90% of our wealth to our children and grandchildren. The balance would go to Charities outlined in our Estate Planning Documents.

FAMILY PHILOSOPHY

At this time in our lives, we both feel that strong values are vital to our family. This includes inner spirituality, meditation, and community commitments.

Additionally, John feels that Ethical (honesty, justice, and fairness), Emotional (compassion, kindness, generosity), Economic (financial responsibility, frugality, stewardship) and Educational (study, self-improvement, academic achievement) values are important.

Jane adds to that list Physical (health, relation, quiet time alone, exercise), Relational (family, friends), Philanthropic (contributions of time and money to care for others) and Recreational (sports, leisure activity, hobbies, family vacations) values.

Among the opportunities that affluence affords us are the ability to help others, personal and family security, and the ability to start, manage, control or invest in business.

The freedom to control all aspects of our lives, the power and influence in society and the ability to become a leader among our peers in responsible wealth management and deployment are additional opportunities that John feels are created through wealth.

Additionally, Jane realizes the opportunity of time to pursue personal spiritual development.

As we impart our philosophy regarding financial stewardship to children and other heirs, we hope they will appreciate the importance of, (1) focus on long-term growth, (2) avoiding deals that appear too good to be true, (3) living within one's means, (4) limiting investments to things that I understand, (5) minimizing the impact of taxes, (6) strategic debt management, (7) focus on investments in a closely held business and (8) giving to charities.

When it comes to transferring family financial values to children and other heirs, we believe it is important to actively discuss the importance of specific financial values, but only to disclose family financial resources when the children have reached financial and emotional maturity. We feel that our children can demonstrate this maturity by age 25. With regard to their specific inheritance, we believe heirs should be informed of their potential legacy around the age of 25 and only after they have demonstrated a level of financial and emotional maturity.

FAMILY LEGACY

We prefer to leave a large enough inheritance so that our children could do anything they want but would still be required to be productive. We feel that parents should offer children the opportunity to become wealthy through responsibility. We believe they will develop more positive values if they are required to contribute to their own financial security.

We are unsure of our children's future ability to manage wealth because of their young age. For this reason, we are concerned about transferring significant wealth to our heirs until we are sure they would manage it responsibly and effectively. To that end, we would like to develop a plan to teach them about managing financial resources.

Given the numerous ways to transfer your family financial values to children and other heirs, we prefer to demonstrate our values by how we lead our daily lives, actively discuss the importance of specific financial values, encourage children to work in order to learn the meaning of money, and become involved as a family in the community.

Our concerns regarding inheritance are (1) if we give our children too large an inheritance, they are likely to lead less productive lives and may even suffer a loss of self-worth, as well as a lack of respect from others, and (2) if we leave a large inheritance to our children, they may spend it unwisely, or otherwise lose it through divorce, lawsuits or poor financial advice. We believe that our children must earn their own wealth, and that as a parent and the wealth holder, we should direct its use toward organizations that will perpetuate our values now and after our deaths. Although we are aware that our children presently feel "entitled" to our wealth, we believe they will get over any disappointment if their inheritance fails to meet their expectations.

SOCIAL CAPITAL LEGACY

Regarding our thoughts on charitable giving, we both feel that as long as our intended family legacy is not compromised, we would consider charitable gifts as part of our estate plan. Jane is actively involved with a charitable organization and plans to continue at her current level of commitment as long as possible, while John would like to increase his involvement as time and money allows. We both feel charitably inclined and would prefer to make our gifts during our lifetimes so that we can enjoy watching the impact of our philanthropy firsthand.

On a scale of 1-10, we rate our overall level of satisfaction with the current effectiveness of our charitable gifts of money and time in improving the well-being of others between a 5 and 8. We currently give a good percentage of our income to various local charities. We both feel that we would like to increase the overall level of our contributions as our net worth increases and we find more time to study and think strategically about our charitable giving.

We are interested in personal or family foundation but would prefer a less complicated alternative to carry out our wishes. Regarding the concept of family philosophy, we want our family involved with us in our charitable activity. However, once we are gone, we would also encourage our children to make decisions on their own regarding philanthropy and to develop their own charitable plans.

In terms of charitable purposes that can benefit from our contributions, we would rank them in order of preference as follows: (1) Spiritual endeavors, (2) Education, (3) Public society benefit, and (4) Human services. It is not important to us to receive recognition for our philanthropic contributions.

SAMPLE CHARITABLE REMAINDER UNITRUST AGREEMENT

The IRS and many charities provide sample language to promote the use of CRTs. This example is provided by the American Cancer Society. This is based on one life, but provisions can be provided for two or more lives. You may contact us at biggerfuture.org for the example to include two lives. Additionally, we have trust examples for many different designs including NIMCRUTs with and without Flip provisions, CRATs, CLTs. Design is important to give you the best tailored solution.

CHARITABLE REMAINDER UNITRUST

On this _____ day of _____, 20 _____, I, _____ (hereinafter "the Donor"), desiring to establish a charitable remainder unitrust within the meaning of Rev. Proc. 2005-52 and §664(d)(2) of the Internal Revenue Code (hereinafter "the Code"), hereby enter into this trust agreement with _____ as the initial trustee (hereinafter "the Trustee").

This trust shall be known as the _____ Charitable Remainder Unitrust.

1. Funding of Trust. The Donor hereby transfers and irrevocably assigns, on the above date, to the Trustee the property described in Schedule A, and the Trustee accepts the property and agrees to hold, manage and distribute the property, and any property subsequently transferred, under the terms set forth in this trust instrument.

2. Payment of Unitrust Amount. In each taxable year of the trust during the unitrust period, the Trustee shall pay to [permissible recipient] (hereinafter "the Recipient") a unitrust amount equal to [a number no less than 5 and no more than 50] percent of the net fair market value of the assets of the trust valued as of the first day of each taxable year of the trust (hereinafter "the valuation date"). The first day of the unitrust period shall be the date property is first transferred to the trust and the last day of the unitrust period shall be the date of the Recipient's death. The unitrust amount shall be paid in equal quarterly installments at the end of each calendar quarter from income and, to the extent income is not sufficient, from principal.

Any income of the trust for a taxable year in excess of the unitrust amount shall be added to principal. If, for any year, the net fair market value of the trust assets is incorrectly determined then, within a reasonable period after the correct value is finally determined, the Trustee shall pay to the Recipient (in the case of an undervaluation) or receive from the Recipient (in the case of an overvaluation) an amount equal to

the difference between the unitrust amount(s) properly payable and the unitrust amount(s) actually paid.

3. Proration of Unitrust Amount. For a short taxable year and for the taxable year during which the unitrust period ends, the Trustee shall prorate on a daily basis the unitrust amount described in paragraph 2 or, if an additional contribution is made to the trust, the unitrust amount described in paragraph 5.

4. Distribution to Charity. At the termination of the unitrust period, the Trustee shall distribute all of the then principal and income of the trust (other than any amount due the Recipient under the terms of this trust) to [designated remainderman] (hereinafter "the Charitable Organization"). If the Charitable Organization is not an organization described in §§170(b)(1)(A), 170(c), 2055(a) and 2522(a) of the Code at the time when any principal or income of the trust is to be distributed to it, then the Trustee shall distribute the then principal and income to one or more organizations described in §§170(b)(1)(A), 170(c), 2055(a) and 2522(a) of the Code as the Trustee shall select, and in the proportions as the Trustee shall decide, in the Trustee's sole discretion.

5. Additional Contributions. If any additional contributions are made to the trust after the initial contribution, the unitrust amount for the year in which any additional contribution is made shall be [same percentage used in paragraph 2] percent of the sum of (a) the net fair market value of the trust assets as of the valuation date (excluding the assets so added and any post-contribution income from, and appreciation on, such assets during that year) and (b) for each additional contribution during the year, the fair market value of the assets so added as of the valuation date (including any post-contribution income from, and appreciation on, such assets through the valuation date) multiplied by a fraction the numerator of which is the number of days in the period that begins with the date of contribution and ends with the earlier of the last day of the taxable year or the last day of the unitrust period and the denominator of which is the number of days in the period that begins with the first day of such taxable year and ends with the earlier of the last day in such taxable year or the last day of the unitrust period. In a taxable year in which an additional contribution is made on or after the valuation date, the assets so added shall be valued as of the date of contribution, without regard to any post-contribution income or appreciation, rather than as of the valuation date.

6. Deferral of the Unitrust Payment Allocable to Testamentary Transfer. All property passing to the trust by reason of the death of the Donor (hereinafter "the testamentary transfer") shall be considered to be a single contribution that is made on the date of the Donor's death. Notwithstanding the provisions of paragraphs 2 and 5 above, the obligation to pay the unitrust amount with respect to the testamentary transfer shall commence with the date of the Donor's death. Nevertheless, payment of the unitrust amount with respect to the testamentary transfer may be deferred from the date of the Donor's death until the end of the taxable year in which the funding of the testamentary transfer is completed. Within a reasonable time after the end of the taxable year in which the testamentary transfer is completed, the Trustee must pay to the Recipient (in the case of an underpayment) or receive from the Recipient (in the case of an overpayment) the difference between any unitrust amounts allocable to the testamentary transfer that were actually paid, plus interest, and the unitrust amounts allocable to the testamentary transfer that were payable, plus interest.

The interest shall be computed for any period at the rate of interest, compounded annually, that the federal income tax regulations under §664 of the Code prescribe for this computation.

7. Unmarketable Assets. Whenever the value of a trust asset must be determined, the Trustee shall determine the value of any assets that are not cash, cash equivalents or other assets that can be readily sold or exchanged for cash or cash equivalents (hereinafter "unmarketable assets"), by either (a) obtaining a current "qualified appraisal" from a "qualified appraiser," as defined in §1.170A-13(c)(3) and §1.170A-13(c)(5) of the Income Tax Regulations, respectively, or (b) ensuring the valuation of these unmarketable assets is performed exclusively by an "independent trustee," within the meaning of §1.664-1(a)(7)(iii) of the Income Tax Regulations.

8. Prohibited Transactions. The Trustee shall not engage in any act of self-dealing within the meaning of §4941(d) of the Code, as modified by §4947(a)(2)(A) of the Code, and shall not make any taxable expenditures within the meaning of §4945(d) of the Code, as modified by §4947(a)(2)(A) of the Code.

9. Taxable Year. The taxable year of the trust shall be the calendar year.

10. Governing Law. The operation of the trust shall be governed by the laws of the State of _____. However, the Trustee is prohibited from exercising any power or discretion granted under said laws that would be inconsistent with the qualification of the trust as a charitable remainder unitrust under §664(d)(2) of the Code and the corresponding regulations.

11. Limited Power of Amendment. This trust is irrevocable. However, the Trustee shall have the power, acting alone, to amend the trust from time to time in any manner required for the sole purpose of ensuring that the trust qualifies and continues to qualify as a charitable remainder unitrust within the meaning of §664(d)(2) of the Code.

12. Investment of Trust Assets. Nothing in this trust instrument shall be construed to restrict the Trustee from investing the trust assets in a manner that could result in the annual realization of a reasonable amount of income or gain from the sale or disposition of trust assets.

13. Definition of Recipient. References to the Recipient in this trust instrument shall be deemed to include the estate of the Recipient with regard to all provisions in this trust instrument that describe amounts payable to and/or due from the Recipient. The prior sentence shall not apply to the determination of the last day of the unitrust period.

IN WITNESS WHEREOF _____and_____
[TRUSTEE] by its duly authorized officer have signed this

agreement the day and year first above written.

_____
[DONOR]

_____
[TRUSTEE]

By _____

[Acknowledgments, witnesses and other execution formalities required by local jurisdiction]

FOR ADDITIONAL RESOURCES go to www.IncreaseYourWorth.org

Made in the USA
Columbia, SC
26 May 2024